Christmas
✦
1995

Christmas ✳ 1995

UNLOCK THE SECRETS TO A TRULY HAPPY HOLIDAY

Mary Thompson and Deborah Pike

Walker and Company
New York

First published in the United States of America in 1995
by Walker Publishing Company, Inc.

Published simultaneously in Canada by
Thomas Allen & Son Canada, Limited, Markham, Ontario

Library of Congress International Standard Serial Number: ISSN pending
ISBN 0-8027-7467-9

Printed in the United States of America

2   4   6   8   10   9   7   5   3   1

Contents

Seizing the Christmas Spirit   1

Tapping Into Tradition
CREATING YOUR OWN CHRISTMAS CUSTOMS   7
Great ideas from around the world; special celebrations for the entire holiday season;
ornament parties; parties for families and singles

Wrapping It Up
NEW TWISTS ON CARDS, TREES, AND DECORATIONS   31
Cards and wrap from UNICEF, Amnesty International, and elsewhere;
natural decorations; what to recycle

Philanthropic Festivities
SPREADING CHRISTMAS CHEER   45
Party ideas that help the needy; themes for teens, families, singles, home, and office;
Angel trees; where to send leftovers

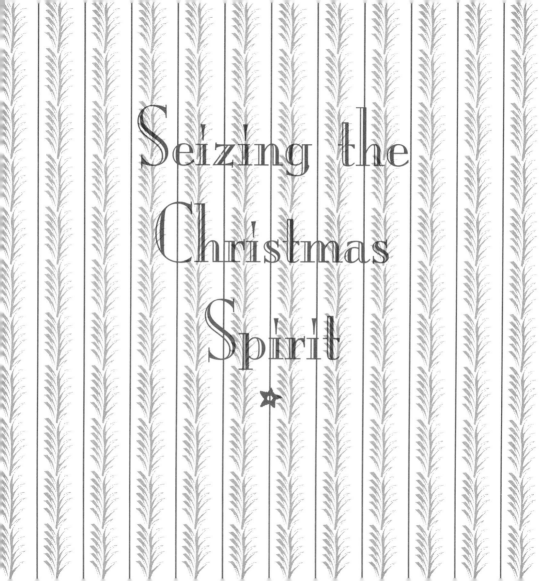

Seizing the Christmas Spirit

For most of us, the onset of the Christmas season brings back a wave of warm memories. Riding high on the crest is family tradition—whether it's a reminiscence of making gingerbread houses, singing carols, or wandering past vibrant window displays. These days, it may seem difficult to recapture the magical feeling that enveloped you as a child, when you patiently listened for the pitter-patter of Santa's reindeer on the rooftop or joyously strung shimmering lights around the Christmas tree. People get caught up in hectic work schedules and office parties, and somewhere between one too many trips to the mall, the spirit of Christmas is forgotten. You're going through the motions— buying presents, baking cookies, and attending parties—but the process becomes mechanical, almost an obligation.

All around us are ads for the "perfect gift," which, more often than not, winds up being a high-tech, expensive gadget. Nowhere to be found are suggestions for getting back to basics: reining in your budget and focusing on the spirit of the holiday. Christmas, you may remember, is a celebration of peace and love, a time for giving and spending time with friends and family. The secret to a happy, more meaningful holiday lies in simplicity and sharing, and *Christmas 1995* is packed with suggestions for seizing the spirit of the season. Among them are ways to share your time — with your community and loved ones. Numerous charitable organizations, and individual families struggling to put food on the table, can use your help especially at this time of the year. Think about how much more rewarding it would be to spend your time assisting someone in need or playing with your kids, rather than dodging shoppers at the mall.

This is not to say there's no place for Christmas gifts; only that it may be time to forego the $4,000 mini notebook computer and $900 golf clubs for something a little more meaningful: your time and company (at a movie or sporting event) or perhaps an inexpensive, more thoughtful present. Spending need not get out of hand. With this in mind, *Christmas 1995* offers suggestions on streamlining your budget and making gifts yourself. A special section on personalized coupons is also included; ideas range from a massage to a night at a concert. There's even a section on presents your children can create. If you don't have the time to make presents, there's still room for creative gift giving; this book provides a comprehensive list of organizations that sell gift items and donate a portion of the proceeds to worthy causes.

Because tradition is, for most people, the backbone of the Christmas season, *Christmas 1995* offers a chapter on creating customs that will last a lifetime. Included are ideas for incorporating charming holiday traditions from around the globe into your festivities. Cooking traditional dishes is another delightful way to make Christmas special; the last chapter of this book serves up suggestions for holiday edibles with an ethnic twist.

Acknowledging the fact that there are different types of households, *Christmas 1995* provides suggestions for singles, couples without children, couples with children (and stepchildren), and single parents. It also takes into account that your circle of friends may come from a variety of backgrounds: You'll find tips on how to share the Christmas spirit with non-Christian pals.

Thanksgiving is a good time to start getting into the Christmas spirit. Get a jump start on your Secret Santa exchange; pick names now, and you'll have a whole month to shop for a gift. Begin your decorating process the day after the last slice of cold turkey is eaten. Set up the lights outside your house right away, rather than waiting till parties get into full swing and time becomes precious. And think about making extra food—breads, pies, and turkey—that can be stowed away until Christmas. Finally, consider serving a Thanksgiving meal at a soup kitchen, food pantry, or emergency nutrition program to launch the Christmas season. Call Foodchain (800) 845-3008 (Atlanta); Second Harvest (800) 532-FOOD (Chicago); or Share Our Strength (800) 969-4SOS (Washington, D.C.) for information on how you can get involved.

Whether the holiday season inspires memories of hurling snowballs in the Christmas tree lot or sitting by the fire and sipping hot chocolate with the faint glow of lights in the background, keep in mind that these moments don't have to be lost to childhood. The spirit of Christmas can be rekindled—in simple, inexpensive, and non-time-consuming ways. Read on.

Tapping Into Tradition

CREATING YOUR OWN
CHRISTMAS CUSTOMS

Although we all share certain Christmas customs—caroling, watching Frosty on TV, opening presents—many rituals are unique to our families. Passed down through the generations, traditions include when to open gifts (on Christmas Eve or Christmas Day), when to serve the large meal, and what food to serve. There is, of course, no right or wrong way to celebrate Christmas. The idea is to do it in a way that's special and appropriate for your family.

Some people don't have a strong Christmas legacy, while others would simply like to start over and invent their own traditions. Consider co-opting foreign customs—whether it's preparing a dish or adopting a ritual. Try taking on traditions from several countries, or stick to your own heritage—whatever strikes your fancy.

❄ For a traditional English holiday, include plum pudding on your Christmas dinner menu (see recipe on page 132), in addition to roast turkey and mince pie. While you're at it, celebrate Stir-Up Sunday, the Sunday before Advent—November 26. (Advent is the season devoted to preparing for Christ's birth.) On this day, family members take turns stirring the pudding—clockwise, with eyes closed—with a wooden spoon (symbolic of Jesus's crib). The stirrer makes a wish, which is supposed to bring good luck.

❄ Two more ideas from England: Bake a loaf of bread on Christmas Eve. According to ancient superstition, one slice will cure all ills. And light the Yule candle; legend has it that it will bring good luck throughout the year.

❄ For a German treat, make lebkuchen, gingerbread, stollen (fruit cake), or marzipan (see recipe on page 133), a popular Christmas goody made from almonds, sugar, and rose water. Consider serving roast pork or roast goose.

❄ More ideas from Germany: If you have children, encourage them to leave their letters to Santa on the windowsill. Sprinkle a little sugar on the letters to make sure Santa doesn't "miss" them, and pick them up while the children are sleeping.

❄ Buy a present for someone and put it in a box surrounded by progressively larger boxes. Mark each box with the name of a family member. As each person takes his or her turn, the packages get smaller and smaller till the right person finally opens the gift. This ritual is meant to bring good fortune to the recipient—provided he or she doesn't know the identity of the gift giver.

❋ Bored with the same old fruitcake? Whip up some Italian *panforte* (a traditional Christmas cake made from hazelnuts, almonds, citron, flour, and spices; see recipe on page 131). Confections with nuts favor fertility, according to farmer folklore.

❋ Re-creating the manger scene is a great family activity. Make this Christmas one to treasure by adding a new twist: set up a crèche or manger scene (including Mary, Joseph, baby Jesus, the Three Kings, angels, and animals) as they do in Italy. Each year, organize a family outing to look for a new figure to enrich it. In Africa, children make manger scenes for friends and neighbors to view on Christmas Day. Although mud bricks are commonly used in Africa, you can construct a scene from paper or clay bricks (or any material you and your kids can get your hands on). Decorate your scene with strings of packing peanuts, bits of metal, plastic, and flashlight bulbs. If visitors like what they see, have them leave a few coins in the dish provided. Finally, encourage your children to put on *pastorellas* (the Mexican word for pageants) showing how the Wise Men and shepherds overcame obstacles to visit Jesus in the manger.

❋ Consider saving a few gifts for your children for Epiphany. This is the day Befana, a witchlike old woman, gives gifts to Italian kids.

❋ If a French holiday catches your fancy here's what you should do: Serve a late supper after church service on Christmas Eve. Include goose or turkey with chestnuts, and serve a yule log cake for dessert. Have your children put their letters to Santa in shoes by the fireplace on Christmas Eve. Then place their gifts in these shoes (or boots—you can fit many more gifts in boots). Decorate the tree with shiny glass balls, tinsel, and artificial snow. Top it off with a star to symbolize the one that guided the shepherds on the night of Jesus's birth.

❋ For a Spanish-style celebration, serve a big dinner on Christmas Eve, including seafood, almond soup, and turkey stuffed with red cabbage, dried fruit, and nuts. Buy a lottery ticket, and if you hold the lucky number, offer part of your winnings to friends and relatives. In Spain, the most famous prize is drawn on December 22.

❋ If you wish to lengthen the holiday season, you might want to adopt the following Scandinavian tradition: On January 13 (known as St. Knut's Day in Sweden, marking the end of the Yuletide season, and Tyvendedagen, or Twentieth Day—the twentieth day after Christmas—in Norway), throw a party to celebrate the final lighting and dismantling of the tree. Let the children eat the cookies and candies used to decorate it.

❄ Another Scandinavian tradition to consider: On Christmas Eve, gather your friends and family around the Christmas tree and join hands. Walk slowly around the tree, singing carols as the Norwegians do, or dance around it as is the Swedish custom. Then open gifts.

❄ Try the Polish tradition of making a honey spice cake or *piernik* (see recipe on page 130). On Christmas Eve, serve fish and babkas (a light, usually cylindrical yeast cake with raisins and often rum). Seat an even number of guests at the table (an odd number signifies bad luck). And—you'll love this one—avoid doing any cooking on Christmas Day. Reheat food or serve it cold, and think about including ham, Polish sausage, and rye bread on your menu.

❄ On Epiphany, serve a large coffee cake with a single almond baked inside, as they do in Poland. Give the piece with the almond in it to the wisest and bravest member of the family; that person becomes the almond king for the year. He or she is designated to protect the family honor and settle quarrels.

❄ For an Irish feast, serve turkey and plum pudding for dinner on Christmas Day. And on Christmas Eve, have your youngest child light a tall candle (called the Christmas candle) and put it in the window. This custom is meant to commemorate the story of Mary and Joseph's search for a room to shelter baby Jesus. Also, put your child's presents in a stocking at the foot of his or her bed.

The following dates have special significance during the Christmas season. Pick one or several and start some new traditions in your household.

November 11: St. Martin's Day

On this day, it's customary to eat goose in preparation for the holiday season. In some countries, children are given small gifts. This holiday originated when Advent lasted for forty days rather than four weeks.

November 25: St. Catherine's Day

A day of festivity for Polish children. On this night boys play games. They each break a branch off a cherry tree, place it in a jug on the windowsill, and care for it. If the branch blossoms by Christmas or New Year's, the boy will supposedly find the sweetheart of his choice the following year.

November 30: St. Andrew's Day or the Feast of St. Andrew
Another day of festivity for Polish children. On the eve of this day, girls play games. Then each girl breaks a twig off a cherry tree and cares for it the same way the boys do. If the twig blossoms by Christmas or New Year's, the girl should receive a marriage proposal.

December 3: First Sunday of Advent
The first of four Advent candles is lit in many churches and households around the world.

December 4: St. Barbara's Day
Barbara, a European martyr and patron saint of miners, is remembered on this day. In many European countries, presents are distributed. Children put shoes out next to their beds, and once they're asleep, family members fill them with chocolate, biscuits, or apples.

December 5: St. Nicholas Eve
In western Europe, the family shares stories about the life of St. Nicholas. St. Nicholas is the patron saint of children, sailors, Russia, pilgrims, and, curiously enough, pawnbrokers. Once the

bishop of Myra, a city in Asia Minor, St. Nicholas was known for his love of children and for his generosity. Over time, the legend of St. Nicholas evolved into what we now know as Santa Claus. To celebrate this night with your family, you might want to get your children together for a special reading of a Christmas story or for a viewing of one of your favorite Christmas movies like *It's a Wonderful Life* or *Miracle on 34th Street*.

December 6: Feast of St. Nicholas

In many countries in western Europe, children put their shoes outside their doors on St. Nicholas Eve, and when they wake up in the morning, the shoes are filled with candy and presents. Add a twist to this celebration: Throw a St. Nicholas Eve party, and invite your friends to bring their old shoes, both dress and athletic. Give the collected goods to a shelter or an organization that distributes clothing to shelters or to people in disaster areas.

December 12: Poinsettia Day

This day is set aside to enjoy the most recognizable Christmas plant. It was brought to the United States in the mid 1800's by an American statesman named Dr. Joel Poinsett. Poinsett served as a member of Congress and as secretary of war.

December 13: St. Lucia Day

This Swedish holiday has both Catholic and pagan origins. Most say that the name is borrowed from the blind martyr St. Lucia. The day marks winter's longest and darkest night. Since the early 1700s, as part of the celebration, a young girl dressed in a white robe and wearing a wreath of lit candles on her head wakes the village or household. She serves coffee and *lussekatter,* a saffron sweet bread, and leads the family or village in singing traditional folk songs.

December 15

In Puerto Rico, this date marks the beginning of Navidades, the official start of the Christmas celebration, which runs through January 6 of the following year. During the holiday, gifts are given on both Christmas Day and Three Kings Day (January 6).

December 16: Posadas Day

This holiday is observed in Mexico and in many Mexican-American communities in the United States. Also known as the "Lodgings," the celebration lasts nine days—until December 24. Since the holiday commemorates the journey of Mary and

Joseph to Bethlehem, communities will often stage a procession of the Holy Family on one of the nine days. Religious ceremonies and festivities, such as the well-known breaking of the piñata, all occur during this time.

December 21: St. Thomas's Day or the Feast of Saint Thomas
This is a good day for charity giving. In England, a candle auction is held. A pin is stuck into a lighted candle, and an auctioneer accepts bids for grazing rights on a piece of land. The last bid received before the pin drops decides who the tenant will be and how much he or she will pay.

December 24: Christmas Eve
On this night, families traditionally gather for meals and gift giving. Many choose to attend religious services on Christmas Eve rather than on Christmas Day. In Austria, there are "Silent Night, Holy Night" celebrations commemorating the creation of this Christmas carol. In Moscow, the bells of St. Basil's Cathedral in Red Square are rung on Christmas Eve. After Lenin's death in 1924, this custom was prohibited by the government for decades; it was resumed in 1990.

December 25: Christmas Day

Christmas was not actually celebrated as a special feast until about the middle of the fourth century, when Rome chose this date to celebrate the Nativity of Christ. There is some debate about whether December 25 was actually the birth date of Christ. It is thought that this date was selected so the Christian celebration would overshadow the pagan festival of Saturnalia, which runs from December 17 through December 23. The ancient Roman festival honors Saturn, the planter god, and was one of the most jubilant celebrations of the time.

December 26: Feast of St. Stephen

This public holiday in Austria is also observed as Boxing Day in the United Kingdom, with the exception of Scotland. Traditionally, gifts were given to workers on Boxing Day. It is now a national holiday in England, Canada, and Wales. In many countries, December 26 is considered the second day of Christmas and is observed as a holiday.

December 27: Feast of St. John

Scandinavians celebrate this occasion by visiting friends and relatives.

December 28: Holy Innocents Day, or Childermas

This day commemorates the slaughter of children in Bethlehem that was ordered by King Herod, who wished to destroy baby Jesus.

December 31: New Year's Eve

Typically a night of revelry welcoming the beginning of a new year (according to the Gregorian calendar).

January 1: New Year's Day

In many countries around the world, January 1 is a public holiday. It is often a day to reflect and make resolutions for the new year.

January 5

Epiphany Eve, also known as Twelfth Night (it's the last of the twelve days of Christmas). This night has a history of celebration and mischievousness.

January 6: Feast of the Epiphany, or Three Kings Day

This day commemorates the Star of Bethlehem leading the Magi, or Three Wise Men, to the manger in Bethlehem. It is also observed as Christmas by the Armenian Church. In some countries, gifts are given because this is the twelfth day after Christmas. It marks the end of the Christmas season. In many countries, decorations must be removed by midnight or bad luck will follow.

Of course, adopting foreign customs is just one way to create your own Christmas traditions. You may have noticed that most apply to families in the classic sense, yet many of us will be celebrating the holiday solo, with stepchildren, or with a spouse. What follows are suggestions aimed specifically at different types of holiday observers: singles, couples without children, families (both traditional and nontraditional—with stepchildren and stepparents), and single parents.

Singles

Getting together with friends is a great way to celebrate the holiday. Consider hosting a holiday "work" party, where you and your guests bake cookies, wrap gifts, and write Christmas cards. Chores are much more fun when you do them with others. Another idea: Have an ornament swap party. Gather your friends and make ornaments, then exchange them. Each ornament will represent a stage of life that you share. If you're more the couch-potato type and don't have the energy to put on a party, head to the video store, pick up some Christmas classics *(Frosty the Snowman, A Charlie Brown Christmas, How the Grinch Stole Christmas, Rudolph the Red-Nosed Reindeer)*, and invite friends over for a screening. Refreshments at any of these get-togethers can be simple: Serve hot chocolate and/or eggnog and—if time permits—Christmas cookies.

If you have a number of non-Christian friends, host a holiday party and tell everyone to bring a dish indicative of their heritage. Jewish friends, for example, can bring latkes (potato pancakes) and challah (an egg-rich bread). Another way to share in each other's holiday traditions: light a menorah with a Jewish friend, then ask him or her to help you decorate your tree. Or, if you plan to exchange gifts, pick a neutral day, such as December 27, and create your own holiday.

So much of what makes Christmas magical is the excitement reflected in children's eyes. Go to the mall or local firehouse and watch kids visiting Santa. (Check their parents' reactions, too.)

Decorate your tree with edible ornaments; then invite neighborhood kids over to eat them the day after Christmas. (You may also be able to get them to help you take down the rest of your ornaments.) One other option: Assist with holiday parties for neighborhood children.

If you're feeling charitable, donate your time to a local organization. Many are short on volunteers during the holidays. Spend an afternoon wrapping presents for underprivileged children; or help shop for, prepare, and deliver meals to people who can't leave their homes. Check the Yellow Pages under social and human services to find out about organizations that provide these services.

Married, Without Children

You and your spouse can have some fun with your holiday cards. Consider sending cards with a photo of you both doing something fun—bungee jumping or just hiking in the mountains. Your friends and family will get a kick out of such a lighthearted greeting. If you're the type to save champagne bottles and corks from special events, mark the corks with the date and occasion and hang them from the branches of your Christmas tree. When you put them up, remind your spouse of the occasion.

As a team, you can repair or paint the home of a needy family; drive a homebound person to a relative's house for Christmas; or help a disabled or elderly individual shop, wrap gifts, or write holiday cards. Again, check the Yellow Pages for listings of local charitable organizations.

Married, with Children

Make each Christmas memorable for your family by encouraging everyone to take part in the birth of a new tradition. This is especially important for "new" families united by a second or third marriage. Doing things together promotes bonding. If your clan is creative, hold a decorating contest. Have each family member come up with one decorating idea (whether it's putting up a certain wreath or using a particular outdoor lighting scheme); then vote on the best idea. Whoever wins gets to be in charge of the decorations. Consider creating the chosen decorations as a family.

Read aloud a different Christmas book every year, and let each child take a turn at picking the book and reading part of it. One suggestion: Whoever picks the book gets to read it.

If your family is active, go on a special holiday outing every year. It could be sleigh riding, sledding, or going to a nearby forest and chopping down a tree—or even just attending a local exhibition, play, or concert. (To find out about local Christmas events, call your city's chamber of commerce or visitors information bureau.)

If music is your thing, tape-record your family singing carols each year. The kids will cherish (and laugh at) the way you sound for years to come.

Theatrical children should be encouraged to put on a Christmas play every year—whether it's one they write themselves or one that involves the original Christmas story. The children can use costumes and props. This is a great way to keep the family in good holiday spirits.

Food-loving families can bond over baking. Consider making a gingerbread house, giving each person his or her own "job" (designing the door, cutting out a window, etc.). Another great bonding opportunity is a cookie-baking day, involving the extended, as well as immediate, family. Several days before Christmas, invite all the aunts, cousins, and grandparents over. Bake from dawn to dusk, and allow everyone to take some cookies home.

To preserve memories from year to year, consider making a home video. Ask similar questions each time, such as: What's unique about this Christmas? What's unique about this year? What is your favorite Christmas? Families that don't own a video camera can rent one for a day or two. If operating a camera is too much of a production, make a holiday scrapbook or journal. Jot down the memories—and mishaps—your family has shared during Christmas. Record the presents exchanged and events attended. Save programs from holiday concerts, photos from Christmas dinner, and letters to Santa. Encourage guests to sign the book. Ask each person to describe a memorable Christmas. Finally, take a holiday photo of your family in the same spot every year—next to the Christmas tree or at the dinner table. You'll be recording the growth of your family.

When giving gifts, consider giving one item routinely. For example, buy an ornament for each member of the family every year, and be sure it signifies a special accomplishment. From year to year, you'll have concrete memories of Christmases past. Another option: buy (or make) the whole family a new ornament each year. As you decorate the tree, you can tell the story of where you got it, why you got it, and what that Christmas was like.

Children, of course, love receiving gifts. So why not extend your Christmas and give them one present for each of the twelve days of Christmas? Or use these twelve occasions to organize family outings, like going window shopping, renting Christmas movies, caroling, decorating the tree, or lighting candles.

Encourage family members to get involved in charitable causes. Ask everyone to pitch in and cook a meal for a needy family, then deliver it together.

A New Family

The suggestions in the preceding section can also be used by blended families. Group activities—such as family outings—are especially appealing because they allow family members to get to know one another better.

Single Parents

Read the section "Married, with Children" for ideas on family activities. If time and money are in short supply, stick to activities that really matter to you, whether it's caroling, decorating the tree, or reading Christmas stories to the children. Focus on one or two things at the most.

If baking is important to you, initiate a cookie exchange with friends. You may not have time to bake a variety of cookies yourself. Be sure that each guest brings a different recipe. When the evening or day is over, you'll have as many types of cookies as guests. If decorating is your forte, consider decking out the children's rooms to get them excited for Christmas. This activity is less time-consuming than attempting to decorate a home's exterior. It may also establish a special holiday bond with your children if they spend the holiday with the other parent. Put ivy and evergreens on their dressers (but be careful not to let your young children eat them), and tie velvet ribbons around their chairs or bedposts. Hang a holiday wreath on the doors to their rooms. Other inexpensive and non-time-consuming activities: Take your children to a recital at a local church or Christmas pageant, or walk (or drive) your children around the neighborhood to admire the lights.

If you aren't able to spend Christmas Day with your children one year, try creating a day-after-Christmas ritual. Make a special breakfast and take the kids ice skating or to see the local tree. The idea of having two Christmases may appeal to them even more.

No matter what type of household you live in, you might consider participating in Operation Santa Claus. Thousands of needy children (and sometimes parents) write letters to this post-office-sponsored program each year. Volunteers write letters back to the children and send donations. For more information, contact your local postmaster or call Operation Santa Claus in New York City, (212) 967-8585. To send a donation, write: Operation Santa Claus, 421 Eighth Avenue, Room 3023, New York, NY 10199-9621.

Wrapping It Up

It Up

New Twists on Cards, Trees, and Decorations

The Christmas spirit often gets lost in the whirlwind weeks beforehand—in eleventh-hour preparations and shopping trips. Instead of waiting till the mad rush begins, sit down after Thanksgiving (you could make the day after Turkey Day a Christmas preparation day) and start making lists: for holiday cards, gifts (noting how much you want to spend on each present), decorations, and other items you need to purchase.

If you're really ambitious, you can start your Christmas shopping as soon as you ring in the new year. Take advantage of all the after-Christmas sales to stock up on discounted cards, wrappings, ornaments, and other extras like napkins, tablecloths, or decorative tins you could use for next year's batches of cookies.

Even if you didn't take advantage of these sales in 1995, keep them in mind for next year. In addition to saving you money, having this done early will free up time for you and your family during the holidays.

For many people, the official start of the Christmas season begins with the Christmas-card list. Sending cards can be an expensive and time-consuming process, so here are a few time- and money-saving ideas.

First, send postcards instead of traditional cards. They're cheaper to mail and can be made by the sender, giving your Christmas salutation a personal touch. Making these can be as simple as getting plain white cards and stamping one side with images of trees or Santas and writing "Happy Holidays" on them. Of course, if you don't have the time or inclination to do this, check out museums, gift shops, or stationery stores for packages of postcards.

You might also want to reduce the size of your list. Sending Christmas cards is a good way to keep in touch with people you don't speak with often, but is it really necessary to send them to those you see on a regular basis? Instead of mailing out lots of cards with just a few words on them, send cards only to the people you see infrequently. Take the time to write a lengthy note about what you've been doing since you last spoke.

If you're exchanging gifts with someone, let your gift serve as your Christmas greeting. If you're throwing a party, let your invitation double as your Christmas card. You could also send New Year's greetings, waiting until you have more time to write personal notes to the recipients. Or double your post-Christmas thank-you notes as holiday greetings and include a form letter about what your family's been up to during the past year.

Remember, during the Christmas season, almost every thing you do (ranging from where you buy your cards and gifts to what kind of party you throw) can be done in a way that benefits some worthy organization. Many of you are already familiar with UNICEF cards, sold by the United Nations Children's Fund to support its health and educational activities around the world.

A box of ten UNICEF Christmas cards costs between $7.50 and $10.00, and half the proceeds go directly to UNICEF programs. The cards are available throughout the country at selected retail outlets such as the home-furnishings retailer Pier 1 Imports, the biggest distributor of UNICEF cards. UNICEF also sells other Christmas necessities, such as wrapping paper and children's toys. So you may be able to do some of your Christmas shopping while ordering your cards. To request a catalog, write to UNICEF, 2515 East Forty-third Street, Chattanooga, TN 37407; call (800) 553-1200; or fax (615) 867-5318. In Canada, write to UNICEF Canada, 443 Mt. Pleasant Road, Toronto, Ontario M4S2LB; call (800) 268-3770; or fax (416) 482-8035.

UNICEF also prints Christmas cards for businesses through its Corporate Card Collection. For information, write to U.S. Committee for UNICEF, Corporate Marketing Department, 333

East Thirty-eighth Street, New York, NY 10016; or call (800) FOR-KIDS. In Canada, contact UNICEF Canada (see page 35).

There are a number of other groups whose work you can support by buying Christmas cards. Purchasing these cards allows you to keep in touch with friends while supporting causes that can make the world a better place.

Amnesty International works to free people who've been wrongly imprisoned and to promote human rights around the world. Its Canadian branch sells Christmas cards as well as T-shirts, jewelry, mugs, and other gift items. For a catalog, write to Amnesty International, Suite 900, 130 Slater Street, Ottawa, Ontario K1P 6E2; or call (613) 563-1891.

The lipstick company M.A.C. sells holiday greeting cards drawn by children who have AIDS. All proceeds go to AIDS charities. Call (800) 387-6707. Also, check out the American Cancer Society's cards. Purchases go toward cancer research. You can even specify what type of research you'd like to support—breast, colon, or pancreatic cancer. Call (212) 586-8700 for more information.

In a rather unusual twist, the Miller Brewing Company also sells Christmas cards. Proceeds from the sale of these cards go to the Thurgood Marshall Scholarship Fund. For more information, call (800) 444-GIVE.

Prophecy Designs sells both printed and braille-embossed greeting cards. A box of eight Christmas cards costs about $9.95. The company also makes large-print cards, which you can send to the visually impaired, and general notecards, which you can give as gifts or use for your own correspondence. The cards feature designs by Prophecy's president and CEO, Kristina Nutting. A percentage of the proceeds is donated to support services for the blind and visually impaired. For more information, write to Prophecy Designs, P.O. Box 84, Round Pond, ME 04564; or call (207) 529-5318.

If you buy cards elsewhere, try to buy those printed on recycled paper. Any way you can cut down on or encourage the recycling of waste during the Christmas season benefits the world you live in.

Perhaps you'll be creating your own Christmas cards. If you have a computer, you can buy software that lets you make professional-looking cards. And if you're lucky enough to have a child who is interested in computers, encourage him or her to help. As for the Christmas greeting, ask family members to come up with poems or sayings that can be used on the cards. Making your Christmas cards a family project could become one of your own holiday traditions.

Kids love to decorate cards, so here are some simple ideas they might try. On one side of a white or colored piece of paper, print a holiday greeting or letter. On the other side have the children paste cutouts of snowflakes, Santas, or trees. Or outline a Christmas scene with glue and have your children sprinkle glitter on the outline. Remember that you'll need to save a place on this side for the recipient's address and fold the paper in half or in thirds so it can be mailed.

Another option: Cut out sponges in the shape of snowmen, Santas, Christmas trees, or words. Have the children sponge-paint the figures or words on white postcards or sheets of paper, and write your Christmas greetings on the other side.

Once the Christmas season is over, don't throw out the cards you received. Instead, send them to St. Jude's Ranch for Children, a residence for abused children. (The address is 100 St. Jude Street, Boulder City, NV 89005.) The children at St. Jude's make new cards out of your old ones and sell the cards to support the ranch. A box of ten cards from St. Jude's costs $6.50, including postage and handling. The nonprofit organization asks that orders for cards be placed at least a month before they are needed because the cards are sent via bulk mail. Three different types of greeting cards are available: religious, nonreligious, and all-occasion. To place an order, call (702) 293-3131.

And don't forget that *you* can use last year's holiday cards; turn them into this year's gift tags. Encourage your children to cut out their favorite pictures from a stack of cards. Use construction paper or grocery bags to mount them.

In addition to cards, trees and decorations are an important part of the Christmas celebration. When you are putting up your tree and decorations, remember to keep four things in mind: Reduce waste, reuse paper, replant trees, and recycle.

Let's start with the Christmas tree. You can use the same tree year after year: Buy a live tree and replant it in your yard after Christmas, then dig it out each year and keep it alive by wrapping the root ball in burlap. Or, if you prefer, buy a live tree and donate it to a local park or forest once the Christmas season is over. Before you decide to do this, call your state or local parks and forestry commission to find out where the tree could be planted after the holidays. You might also want to check with other organizations like libraries, churches, or schools that might appreciate a new tree as part of their landscape.

Many states have parks where you can chop down your own tree. This expedition can become a Christmas tradition for your family or for you and a group of friends. Call your state forestry office for the names of tree farms.

If you do opt for a cut tree, remember to mulch it once you take it down. (Your local or county recycling office should have information on where this can be done.) Other possibilities are to use the tree for firewood or as a bird feeder: On the tree, hang some pinecones covered with peanut butter and birdseed for your feathered friends to feed on during the winter months.

When you decorate your tree and home, think about using natural, instead of store-bought, decorations. A walk through the woods can provide you with many things to make your home and tree more festive. Greens can be gathered for the mantle and staircases. Pinecones can be spray-painted silver and gold and hung from your Christmas tree or placed on the mantle or the Christmas table among a bunch of greens. You can also make your own swags or wreaths with the greens.

When you're sifting through your ornaments, keep this in

mind: the simpler, the better. Pare down your collection; use only the ones with a common theme (like Santas or angels) or made of the same material (like felt). Put bows or garlands in one color on the rest of the tree. And rather than buying new decorations, ask your kids to help you fix up the ones you already have. Add fresh ribbon to a wreath; put a new coat of paint on chipped ornaments. Use old-fashioned decorations like strings of popcorn or cranberries to decorate your tree. (Forget tinsel—it's messy and can't be reused or recycled.) Add white lights and some candy canes, and you have a beautiful tree that can be re-created each year just by buying new candy canes.

Get your children involved in the decorating process. Have them cut out paper snowflakes to be hung from the tree, or decorate walnut shells with Santa faces by gluing on cotton for a beard and adding a little red felt hat. Seashells collected at the beach during the summer can be spray-painted and hung from your tree as ornaments.

Break out your cookie cutters, and have the children trace gingerbread figures and stars to cut out and cover with glitter, fingerpaints, or cutouts from magazines. Pull a string through the top of these decorations, and add them to your tree. Gather up any small gift boxes, and have your children wrap them to hang as little presents from your tree.

If you have old screens that are ripped and can no longer be used on your windows, consider cutting them up and using the pieces for decorations. Small cones can be shaped from the screens and covered with greens or construction paper and decorated as mini Christmas trees. You can also form bows from the screens, spray-paint them gold or silver, and hang them from your tree.

Though typically associated with the Easter season, decorated eggs can be used during Christmas as well. Dye them red or green, or have your children paint or decorate them with glitter and ribbon.

Gift wrappings can also be placed in the category of decorations. These need not be expensive to be effective. Remember, the wrapping will probably be thrown away once the presents are opened. Nevertheless, spending a little time to make gifts look special can make them all the more memorable.

You don't need to buy rolls of expensive wrapping paper each year. Instead, be creative. Wrapping paper can be a humble paper bag covered with stickers, paint, or candies. It can also be white butcher paper tied with a velvet or plaid ribbon. Children's drawings can be used for packaging. So can the Sunday comics, waxed paper or tissue, scarves or handkerchiefs, and old magazines. Tailor your wrapping to the gift you're giving; if it's a piece of trendy clothing, wrap it in a spread from a fashion magazine. Take advantage of your children's artistic talents and have them make their own gift wrap.

Be creative, too, when wrapping food gifts. Use a festive coffee mug or hatbox. Look for unusually shaped boxes.

A final note on gift wrap: Don't forget that many of the nonprofit organizations mentioned earlier in this chapter sell wrapping paper as well as Christmas cards.

Do you know that you can recycle a lot of the packing used to protect presents? The Association of Foam Packaging Recyclers has information about where you can take different packing materials to be recycled. For more information, call (800) 828-2214. Also, many franchises of the alternative mail service Mail Boxes Etc. will accept Styrofoam packing for recycling.

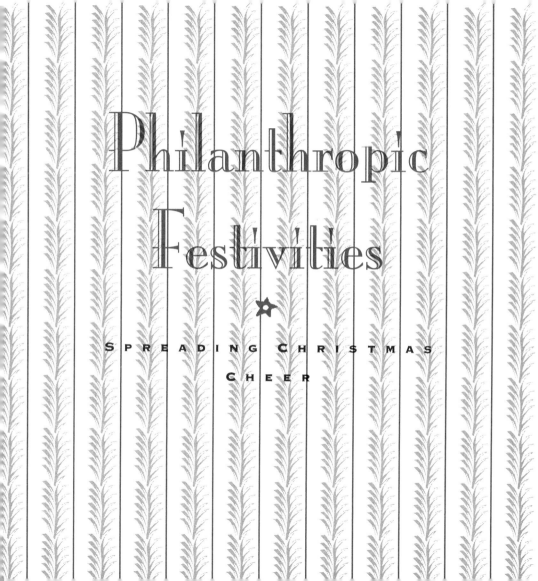

Philanthropic Festivities

✦

SPREADING CHRISTMAS CHEER

The holidays provide a great excuse for a party. Most people's calendars are crammed with office functions and open houses throughout the month of December. Parties can be more than drinking and eating and catching up with old acquaintances. They are perfect occasions for celebrating the season of giving.

As you know, there is power in numbers. What can twenty people do that two people can't? Put on a Christmas dinner complete with gifts for a family that can't afford Christmas. A big group of people can also serve a full dinner shift at a homeless shelter or bring dinners to those not able to leave their homes.

Rally your friends and family and get them to give their time to others at Christmas rather than buying you or your loved ones gifts. Throw a party that will help a needy family or a good cause. Include your children and their friends to remind them of the true spirit of Christmas.

There are a number of ways a Christmas get-together can be a catalyst for charitable giving. The following are a few examples of how you, your friends and family and coworkers can bring Christmas cheer to those who are less fortunate.

✳ Have friends over for dinner or drinks, but stipulate on the invitation that they bring a wrapped present for a needy child, with the sex and age of the intended recipient on it. Set a dollar limit on the gift. Donate the presents to a toy drive or charitable organization collecting gifts during the holiday season. Check with churches to see if they know of families to whom the gifts could be donated.

You can also give gifts to needy children through the Salvation Army's "Angel Trees." These can be found in malls, post offices, and banks at Christmastime. The trees are decorated with paper angels, each of which bears a child's name, age, sex, size, and a gift suggestion. Ask your guests to pick an angel and buy the present specified, which will be put under the tree and distributed by the Salvation Army. Your local chapter of the Salvation Army can give you more information on this innovative toy drive.

✳ If you would rather give something other than presents, consider holding a mini food drive. This is an especially good idea if you are having an open house with a lot of guests. Ask them to bring canned or packaged food to the party. The collection can then be donated to schools, churches, or other organizations that are sponsoring food drives during the season.

✳ If you have a close group of friends with whom you typically exchange presents, try something different this year. Put on a Christmas dinner for a family who can't afford to have one. The cost of putting on one of these feasts, split between a group of people, would probably not be any more than buying each other gifts. With a larger group of friends, you could also get gifts for the family's children.

You might want to try this idea out at the office. Put on a dinner for a needy family instead of exchanging Secret Santa gifts among your coworkers. Check with shelters and churches about sponsoring a family at Christmas.

✳ If you have a teen at home during the school break, encourage him or her to get a group of friends together to shovel snow, run errands, or do chores for elderly or homebound neighbors. Afterward, invite them inside for a couple of movies or a marathon session of MTV.

✳ Instead of exchanging gifts with members of your extended family, have each person give $20 to a pool. Then throw all the family members' names into a hat, and let the person whose name is chosen donate the money to the charity of his or her choice.

✳ A group of twelve friends can celebrate the twelve days of

Christmas as follows: Get together for dinner before the beginning of the Christmas rush, and think up twelve ways you can spread Christmas cheer through a donation of your time or money. For example, one person could serve dinner one night at a homeless shelter, another could read books to nursing-home residents. How about one of you taking an underprivileged child to see a movie or a Christmas show, or buying a book for a library, giving money to a local charity, or giving blood? Once you've come up with twelve ideas, write them down on twelve slips of paper, throw the slips into a hat, and have each person choose one. Carrying out these charitable activities can be your Christmas gifts to one another.

❋ Throw a caroling party. Photocopy a number of carols, and staple them together in a booklet. Then go around your neighborhood or to a local nursing home. Pass out disposable cameras to all so everyone can record the day's—or night's—events.

❋ For your younger children and their friends, hold a "Junior Santa" party. Have the children bring toys that they've outgrown but which are still in good condition. At the party, clean the toys and have the children wrap and label them. Then donate them to a hospital, orphanage, or a group collecting Christmas gifts for needy children.

❄ Have your friends over for a baking party. Do you know of a church or school that's having a bake sale? A group that's selling food at a fair to raise money during the season? Get your friends together for a night of baking and decorating Christmas cookies or bread, and donate the finished goods to the sale.

❄ A party with a book theme can help your local library. Find out what books the library has ordered or is planning to order. Make a list of these books, and assign each of your guests to buy a book or donate the money for the book to the library. Try to match each person's interests with the book he or she will responsible for. In addition, invite your guests to bring some of their old books to the party so they can be given to a worthy organization, such as a library, shelter for the homeless, or home for battered women.

❄ Buy a tree for a family who can't afford one, and invite your friends and family over to decorate it with ornaments they have bought for this occasion. You supply the tinsel and the lights, and have a few members of the group deliver and set up the tree.

There are couple of other ideas you may want to consider as themes for your party—or as traditions you can initiate at your office, in your neighborhood, or among your friends. During the holiday season, participating Lenscrafters outlets will take used eyeglasses, clean them up, and note their prescription. The specs will then be distributed to people in developing countries who need eyeglasses. Put a note up in your office or around your neighborhood and see if you can get people to donate their old glasses. For more information about the program, call (800) 522-LENS.

Your neighborhood dry cleaner may participate in a "Coats for Kids" program. Through this program, you can donate the coats your children have outgrown. The dry cleaners will clean the coats and give them to a local charity, which will distribute them to needy children. Ask your dry cleaner if it participates in this program, or check with a local dry cleaners association.

Even if your Christmas party does not revolve around doing something for others, you can still help out charitable organizations. For example, if you are having a party at your home or office, there's a number you can call to find out where you can donate leftover food to a homeless shelter or a home for battered families. Call Foodchain at (800) 845-3008, Monday through Friday between the hours of 8:30 A.M. and 4:30 P.M. (EST). This organization will be able to direct you to a shelter or organization that could use the food.

Gifts that Keep on Giving

CONSIDER CHARITABLE DONATIONS

You can probably remember a time when the excitement of Christmas meant the anticipation of a special gift. Each year, you'd scan the TV ads and toy stores in search of what Santa could bring. But as you grow older, you realize there's more to the spirit of giving than a toy or a game. You begin to question the time and expense, all the frenetic spending that goes on during the holiday season. Although you may not want to skimp on the presents for your children or nieces and nephews, you may prefer to take a different approach to the gifts you give to the adults on your Christmas list.

One approach is to give to a friend's favorite charity (or a charity reflecting a friend's passionate interest) in lieu of buying him or her a gift. Giving to a charity or nonprofit organization can help spread the message of the season beyond your own circle. Earmark your contribution; if your friend is an ardent feminist and volunteers at a women's shelter, ask that the administrators of a women's group use your donation specifically for women's shelters. When you write the check, include a letter that gives your friend's name and address and ask that the group notify her or him of the gift.

Before sending in your check, learn how your donations will be used. What percentage of the money goes to the organization's services? What percentage goes to administration? Organizations that funnel more money into their administrative activities than into delivering the education, medical care, or food they purport to may not be as effective in carrying out their goals. Also ask what kind of functions your money will support. Do you endorse these sorts of activities? Do your friends agree with the purpose of this group? Double-check how the funds are used, and ask for a financial statement or an annual report.

When making a donation, don't send cash or use your credit card. And don't forget to keep clear records of your donations since they are often tax deductible.

What follows is a list of charities, mostly taken from the Council of Better Business Bureau's *Annual Charity Index*. (The remainder were highly rated by the American Institute of Philanthropy.) The charities on the list meet all twenty-two standards set out by the CBBB. These standards include public accountability, use of funds, solicitations and informational materials, fund-raising practices and governance. To receive a copy of the *Annual Charity Index*, send a check or money order for $12.95, made payable to the Council of Better Business Bureaus, to:

Charity Index, Council of Better Business Bureaus, 4200 Wilson Boulevard, Suite 800, Arlington, VA 22203; or call (703) 276-0100.

The CBBB's *Index* lists the charities that the CBBB's Philanthropic Advisory Service most frequently receives inquiries about. It does not, however, indicate which charities meet all of the CBBB's standards. To get an up-to-date list of those organizations that do meet the CBBB's criteria, order a copy of the CBBB's *Give But Give Wisely*, a bimonthly publication that provides information and guidance about charitable giving. Or order the *Charity Rating Guide*, published by the American Institute of Philanthropy (AIP), for $3. Write to: American Institute of Philanthropy, 4579 Laclede Avenue, Suite 136, St. Louis, MO 63108; or call (314) 454-3040.

The following charities are by no means the only organizations where your money will be used wisely. Don't forget your local library, schools, hospitals, police and firefighters' groups, or local parks at Christmastime. A number of wonderful and deserving organizations may not have been included in the CBBB's publications because they are local rather than national. Ask your state or local divison of the CBBB or AIP if it has information on local charities you're interested in supporting. Also check the charity indexes at your local library.

The list that follows is broken down into nine categories: animal and wildlife groups; children's groups; environmental groups; health organizations involved in both research and education; human services groups, which provide counseling, crisis care, as well as assistance for the disabled; international relief organizations; veterans' groups; women's groups; and other organizations, including those involved in education, civil rights, food, housing, and drug abuse.

Animal and Wildlife Groups

Animal Legal Defense Fund, 1363 Lincoln Avenue, Suite 7, San Rafael, CA 94901; (415) 459-0885.
Protects and promotes animal rights.

Defenders of Wildlife, 1224 Nineteenth Street, NW, Washington, DC 20036; (202) 659-9510.

Educates the public about wildlife issues, as well as protects endangered species and their habitats.

Humane Society of the United States, 2100 L Street, NW, Washington, DC 20037; (202) 452-1100.

Improves the quality of life for all livestock, wildlife, laboratory animals, and pets on local, regional, and national levels.

Wildlife Habitat Canada, 1704 Carling Avenue, Suite 301, Ottawa, Ontario, Canada K2A 1C7; (613) 722-2090.

Works with private landowners, governmental, and nongovernmental organizations to protect Canada's wildlife by conserving animal habitats.

Children's Groups

Boys and Girls Clubs of America, 771 First Avenue, New York, NY 10017; (212) 351-5900.

Provides advisory services to community groups that sponsor programs for young people in recreation, job training, and prevention of alcohol and drug abuse.

Boys Town/Father Flanagan's Boys' Home, 14100 Crawford Street, Boys Town, NE 68010; (402) 498-1300.

Gives food, clothing, shelter, education, spiritual guidance, and medical care to abused, handicapped, and homeless youth.

Children Incorporated, 1000 Westover Road, Richmond, VA 23220; (804) 359-4562.

Provides food, clothing, shelter, education, and medical assistance to needy children in the United States and overseas.

Children's Defense Fund, 25 E Street, NW, Washington, DC 20001; (202) 628-8787.

Provides a voice for the children of America. Works with state governments to initiate new programs and expand and update old ones in the areas of child care, child development, education, adolescent pregnancy prevention, family support, and mental health.

Make a Wish Foundation, 100 West Clarendon, Suite 2200, Phoenix, AZ 85013; (800) 722-9474.

Grants wishes to children under the age of eighteen who have life-threatening illnesses.

Environmental Groups

Canadian Parks and Wilderness Society, Wildlands League, 160 Bloor Street East, Suite 1335, Toronto, Ontario, Canada M4W 1B9; (416) 324-9760.

Protects Canada's parks and wilderness areas.

Center for Marine Conservation, 1725 DeSales Street, NW, Suite 500, Washington, DC 20036; (202) 429-5609.

Conserves marine habitats, prevents marine pollution, and protects endangered marine life.

National Arbor Day Foundation, 211 N. Twelfth Street, Suite 501, Lincoln, NE 68508; (402) 474-5655.

Encourages tree planting and educates people about the conservation of trees throughout America.

Nature Conservancy, 1815 North Lynn Street, Arlington, VA 22209; (703) 841-5300.

Preserves rare and endangered species by protecting natural land and waters.

Wilderness Society, 900 Seventeenth Street, NW, Washington, DC 20006; (202) 833-2300.

Strives to preserve wilderness and wildlife in America and to gain support for environmental issues.

Health Organizations

American Foundation for AIDS Research, 733 Third Avenue, New York, NY 10017; (212) 682-7440.

Supports HIV/AIDS-related biomedical research and awards grants to promote HIV/AIDS prevention.

American Institute for Cancer Research, 1759 R Street, NW, Washington, DC 20009; (202) 328-7744.

Educates the public about cancer. Also funds research on the causes and treatments of the disease, specifically the link between cancer and diet.

American Kidney Fund, 6110 Executive Boulevard, Suite 1010, Rockville, MD 20852; (800) 638-8299.

Provides direct financial assistance, educational programs, research grants, and community services for people with kidney disease.

Leukemia Society of America, 600 Third Avenue, New York, NY 10016; (212) 573-8484.

Promotes and supports research into causes, cures, and treatments for leukemia and related diseases.

National Multiple Sclerosis Society, 733 Third Avenue, New York, NY 10017; (212) 986-3240.

Works to prevent, treat, and cure MS and to improve the quality of life for both individuals with MS and their families.

Human Services Groups

The Association for Retarded Citizens of the U.S./The ARC, 500 East Border Street, Suite 300, Arlington, TX 76010; (817) 261-6003.

Strives to improve the welfare of the mentally retarded and their families, as well as to reduce the incidence of mental retardation.

Covenant House, 346 West Seventeenth Street, New York, NY 10011; (212) 727-4000.

Provides crisis care to homeless and runaway youths under twenty-one years of age.

Guiding Eyes for the Blind, 611 Granite Springs Road, Yorktown Heights, NY 10598; (914) 254-4024.

Works to provide greater mobility for visually handicapped people through professionally trained guidedogs.

Mays Mission for the Handicapped, 604 Colonial Drive, Heber Springs, AR 72543; (501) 362-7526.

Provides employment and other services for handicapped people, along with spiritual guidance.

International Relief Organizations

Americares Foundation, 161 Cherry Street, New Canaan, CT 06840; (203) 966-5195.

Gives emergency relief and medical aid to communities around the world in need of disaster relief.

International Church Relief Fund, 182 Farmers Lane, Santa Rosa, CA 95405; (707) 528-8000.
Provides nutritional, medical, and material support and disaster relief to underdeveloped countries.

Map International, 2200 Glynco Parkway, P.O. Box 50, Brunswick, GA 31521; (912) 265-6010.
Supplies emergency relief to other countries. Also helps develop assistance projects for missions in developing countries and provides health-related workers with short-term overseas service projects.

World Relief Corporation, P.O. Box WRC, Wheaton, IL 60189; (708) 665-0235.
Helps people in developing countries through relief and development projects. Also provides food, clothing, and medicine.

Veterans' Groups

Amvets National Service Foundation, 4647 Forbes Boulevard, Lanham, MD 20706; (301) 459-6181.

Provides financial aid for Amvets' programs, the goals of which are to help American veterans and their families.

Blinded Veterans Association, 477 H Street, NW, Washington, DC 20001; (202) 371-8880.

Promotes the welfare of blind and visually impaired veterans of the U.S. Armed Forces.

Women's Groups

Ms. Foundation for Women, 141 Fifth Avenue, New York, NY 10010; (212) 353-8580.

Supports the empowerment of women and girls in the United States. Also provides financial and technical assistance to grassroots women's projects and promotes public consciousness of women's issues.

National Organization for Women (NOW), 1000 Sixteenth Street, NW, Washington, DC 20036; (202) 331-0066.

Works to advance women's rights.

Other Organizations

Amnesty International. In the United States: 322 Eighth Avenue, New York, NY 10001; (800) AMNESTY. In Canada: 130 Slater Street, Suite 900, Ottawa, Ontario K1P 6E2; (613) 563-1891.

Works to release people who've been imprisoned because of race, religion, sex, age, or beliefs. Also attempts to improve prison conditions and to abolish torture and execution.

Association of American Indian Affairs, 245 Fifth Avenue, New York, NY 10016; (212) 689-8720.

Promotes the welfare of Native Americans and Alaska Natives by protecting their rights, natural resources, and by improving their health, education, and economic development.

Christian Appalachian Project, 322 Crab Orchard Road, Lancaster, KY 40446; (606) 792-3051.

Provides social and economic programs to the underprivileged in Appalachia through education, job training, and emergency aid.

National Trust for Historic Preservation, 1785 Massachusetts Avenue, NW, Washington, DC 20036; (202) 673-4000.
Works to promote American heritage and to help preserve historic buildings, objects, and communities.

In addition to the above suggestions, many other organizations could use your donation at Christmas and throughout the year. Some fund research for or work with people with cancer, muscular dystrophy, and cerebral palsy. And don't forget to check out local charities and smaller nonprofit institutions.

Another source for charitable giving is the *Alternative Gift Catalog*, published by Alternative Gift Markets, an interfaith, nonprofit Christian ministry. The catalog profiles a number of charitable organizations to which you can make specific donations. Among the worthy projects: preserving one acre of rain forest, providing literacy and hygiene training for a person in Nepal, giving job counseling to a homeless person in the United

States, or providing tuition for schoolchildren in Haiti. For a copy of the catalog, write to: Alternative Gift Markets, Inc., 20646 Highway 18, Apple Valley, CA 92307; or call (800) 842-2243.

Let the Shopping Begin

Begin

At Retailers with a Conscience

When you're thinking about where to start Christmas shopping, your first thought might be "at the mall." But keep in mind you can make your money go farther by buying gifts from organizations that sell goods to raise money for the causes they support, like protecting the environment or working for human rights. Many groups sell reasonably priced goods, with part of each sale's proceeds going to support the group's activities or other nonprofit organizations whose work the group endorses.

Because thrift is one of the themes of this book, the catalogs recommended here sell gifts that are typically under $20, though there are a few that come in a little higher. Also included are retailers that sell environmentally friendly goods because buying these goods helps keep the world a little cleaner.

These mail-order retailers donate a portion of their profits to their own work or that of other nonprofit organizations. Some may have outlets near you, but if they don't, refer to the phone numbers provided to request a copy of their catalog. Remember, if you're shopping by mail, start early.

All Things Wise and Wonderful, Inc., P.O. Box 267, Pierrefonds Station, Pierrefonds, Quebec, Canada H9H 4K9; (514) 683-8407.

You have to send C$2 to receive this catalog, but that money is refunded with your first order. All Things Wise and Wonderful sells environmentally friendly products ranging from nightshirts to crystal stone deodorants. It also stocks gourmet foods, cosmetics, and natural insect repellents. It's a "green" general store with plenty of reasonably priced products that would be welcomed by many of your friends.

The Art Institute of Chicago, The Museum Shop, 111 South Michigan Avenue, Chicago, IL 60603-6110; (800) 621-9337.

The Art Institute is a great source for Christmas cards and gifts. It sells cards, jewelry, books, and prints for under $20. It also sells a beautiful Advent calendar—a perfect gift for the season. (Don't forget to stop by the museums in smaller towns as well as big cities. And remember that museum memberships make great gifts; consider giving one to an art-loving family or friend.)

Better Homes Foundation; (800) 962-4676.

At Christmastime, the Better Homes Foundation sells a couple of products, the proceeds of which fund its work to place homeless families in permanent housing. For example, it sells beeswax candles made by homeless people. These candles cost under $10 for a box of two eight-inch candles, and almost half the purchase price goes to support the foundation's work. The gifts may change from year to year, so call the toll-free number to see what is on the foundation's list for Christmas 1995, or pick up an issue of *Better Homes and Gardens*, where you can find pictures of and prices for the goods.

The Body Shop Catalog, The Body Shop by Mail, 452 Horsehill Road, Cedar Knolls, NJ 07927-2014; (800) 541-2535.

The Body Shop sells soaps, creams, brushes, bath products, makeup, and other personal-care products. Prices vary depending on the product, but many goods are priced under $20.

Some of the profits go toward helping communities around the world, either by supporting new business initiatives or by providing educational programs for the company's employees and its customers. The Body Shop also supports nonprofit organizations like Amnesty International, which works to free people who have been wrongly imprisoned. In addition, Body Shop customers are encouraged to bring in their used bottles for refills to cut down on waste. Finally, the company's products are minimally packaged, also helping to preserve the environment.

When you finish with the catalog, the company asks that you pass it on to a friend or bring it to one of its stores to be recycled.

Bridgehead, 20 James Street, Ottawa, Ontario, Canada K2P 0T6; (800) 565-8563; fax (613) 567-1468.

Bridgehead is an arm of Oxfam-Canada, a nonprofit organization devoted to educating the public about world hunger and to setting up self-development and disaster relief programs in Africa, Asia, Latin America, and the Caribbean. Bridgehead sells goods made in Third World countries. Its catalog features gift items like jewelry, clothing, and toys, as well as greeting cards.

The Company of Women, 102 Main Street, Nyack, NY 10960-0742; (800) 937-1193.

Proceeds from the sale of products ordered through this catalog generate funds for the programs of the Rockland, New York,

Family Shelter. This is an agency serving victims of domestic violence, rape survivors, and the homeless. Gifts range from clocks to pillows, from T-shirts (printed with inspirational messages) to security devices.

Co-op America, 1850 M Street NW, Suite 700, P.O. Box 18217, Washington DC 20036; (202) 223-1881.

Co-op America's catalog features a number of goods made by a variety of projects around the world. These projects work with small businesses to foster rural economic development. They also help Native Americans establish economic independence by creating and developing small businesses. Profits from the sales also go to groups that teach job skills to homeless people and to those that set up alternative trade organizations in developing countries. (You can buy the trade organizations' products through the catalog.) In addition, Co-op America features a number of environmentally friendly products.

Because many of the goods are handmade and imported, Co-op America asks that you do your Christmas ordering by November 30 so your items will arrive in time for the holidays.

The products the catalog sells range from clothes to food to "green" underwear, all for under $20. Remember that depending on what you buy, proceeds from your purchase will go to support the business that produced it. For example, the Women's Bean Project in Denver, which provides jobs and job training for homeless women in that city, sells soup mixes and pasta salad ingredients. Each of these products comes dried in its own wooden box, complete with recipes.

The catalog also features T-shirts, books, and other goods, all of which are made by people trying to better their lives, groups supporting budding economies, and organizations working to preserve the environment.

Earth General, 72 Seventh Avenue, Brooklyn, NY 11217-3649; (800) 562-2203, in New York City (718) 398-4648.

Through its store and catalog, Earth General sells a variety of environmentally friendly products, ranging from untreated, organic bedding to recycled glassware. For under $20, you can buy natural cotton dishtowels, potholders, aprons, or reusable lunchbags. For children, there are a number of games, as well as paper-making kits, wooden toys, coloring books, and natural crayon sets. Earth General also sells candles made by Light Up America, a New York–based organization that employs homeless people. Proceeds from the sale of these candles go toward refurbishing abandoned houses to house the homeless.

EPI Marketing, 250 Pequot Avenue, Southport, CT 06490; (800) WHALE93 or (203) 255-1112.

When you buy a gift made by EPI Marketing, 5 to 20 percent of the proceeds from the sale will be donated to conservation groups so that they can continue their work. The groups EPI supports are the Nature Conservancy, the World Wildlife Fund, the Earth Island Institute, and the United States Fish and Wildlife Service. EPI Marketing sells Earthmates, reversible stuffed animals that can be turned into globes. By buying one stuffed animal you will help preserve twenty-five square feet of endangered rain-forest habitat or generate funds for the Earth Island Institute or the International Wildlife Coalition. How your money is used depends on whether you buy a Jurassic Dino Globe, a dolphin, whale, polar bear, or monkey.

EPI Marketing also sells, among other things, coffee mugs and whale adoption kits.

Forestsaver, Inc., P.O. Box 610264, Bayside, NY 11361; (800) 777-9886.

Forestsaver sells MAPelopes, which are colorful stationery and envelopes made from surplus maps. One set includes fifty-five sheets of stationery, eighteen envelopes, and twenty-eight address labels. In addition, the company sells journals, coloring books, gift wrap, and eco-writer pencils which are made from 100 percent recycled cardboard and paper. Save a tree, and get these goods for the letter writers on your list.

The Metropolitan Museum of Art, 255 Gracie Station, New York, NY 10028-9998; (800) 468-7376.

Another great source for sophisticated but inexpensive gifts. Posters for budding artists, Christmas cards, silver candle snuffers, dishes, address books, and games are all available through this catalog for less than $20.

National Wildlife Federation, 1400 Sixteenth Street, NW, Washington DC 20077-9964; (800) 432-6564.

The NWF sells T-shirts, mugs, jewelry, and games for the children and teenagers on your list. A child would probably appreciate a subscription to the two magazines published by the NWF. *Your Big Back Yard* is an activity magazine for children ages three to five, and *Ranger Rick,* a publication for school-age children, qualifies the young subscriber for a junior membership in the NWF.

The Paper Source, General Delivery, Fallbrook, Ontario, Canada K0G 1A0; (800) 665-1143 or (613) 267-7191.

If you give stationery to a friend or family member, make sure it's made of recycled paper. You don't need to look any farther than this catalog to find note paper, cards, office paper, and envelopes for the people on your list. The Paper Source also sells Christmas cards.

Royal Ontario Museum, 100 Queen's Park, Toronto, Ontario, Canada M4S 2C6; (416) 586-5842.

Each September the museum publishes a catalog for the Christmas season. It sells prints, posters, and jewelry, as well as glassware, games, and toys.

Signals, WGBH Educational Foundation, P.O. Box 64428, St. Paul, MN 55164-0428; (800) 669-9696.

This catalog is a publication of WGBH Educational Foundation in Boston, which supports public television. It has a wonderful selection of videos to choose from, including classic PBS productions of *The Scarlet Pimpernel* and *The Merchant of Venice.* It also sells videos by British star John Cleese, such as the *How to Irritate People Video* and *John Cleese: The Strange Case of the End of Civilization Video.*

Starbucks Coffee, 2203 Airport Way South, P.O. Box 34510, Seattle, WA 98124-1510; (800) 782-7282.

Starbucks offers a wide variety of coffees, as well as coffee-making and drinking paraphernalia you can send to the java lovers on your list. It's included in this section because it has the perfect gift for those who are interested in spreading the wealth around. Starbucks CARE Sampler features four half-pound bags of coffee from the different countries Starbucks and CARE (the world's largest international aid and development organization) have been working with. Starbucks donates $2 to CARE for each Starbucks CARE Sampler sold. So keep this company in mind for the adults on your list.

Very Special Arts, Very Special Arts Holiday Collection, P.O. Box 428, Taylor, MI 48180; (800) 866-8VSA.

Very Special Arts is an international organization that offers programs in the arts for disabled individuals. VSA has programs in fifty-five countries and works to promote awareness of the educational and cultural benefits of the arts for all people. Its holiday catalog features Christmas ornaments made by participants in the VSA programs in India, holiday notecards featuring the artwork of VSA artists, and T-shirts printed with the work of artists who work with VSA.

Remember that some of the other organizations mentioned earlier, like UNICEF and Amnesty International, sell gifts through their catalogs as well.

Cheap, Cheerful, and Creative

✳

GIFTS FOR UNDER $20

Charitable donations and products purchased through retailers who donate a portion of their proceeds will light up the faces of some people on your list but not others. Fortunately, there's a slew of other inexpensive options.

When you embark on your shopping journey, use your imagination. Expense is no substitute for creativity or thoughtfulness. Keep in mind what people need but might not have bought themselves. What are their hobbies or interests? Is there something you could buy them that would encourage them to begin a hobby?

Before you go out to buy the gifts, make a list of all the people you need to buy presents for. Then list two or three gifts you feel would be appropriate for each person. Getting an idea of what you're looking for beforehand will save you time and probably money, because you won't end up reaching for an expensive item as a last-minute substitute. Once you've gotten your list together, call stores ahead of time to find out whether they have the item. Don't forget to ask the price.

If you're stumped by what to get certain people on your list, consider buying "standby" gifts like books or videos, or making a batch of cookies delivered in a new tin or cookie jar that can be used again. Framed photographs are always welcome, as are Christmas ornaments or other decorative items that can be used during the holiday.

It's important to establish a dollar limit before starting to shop. Avoid using credit cards; if you must, choose one low-interest card and stick to it. Consider opening a mutual fund, interest-bearing savings account, or one-year CD to save money for next Christmas.

To save yourself time during Christmas, and to avoid the Christmas rush, buy gifts throughout the year. And keep an eye out for decorative containers, pretty jars, or tins you can use to package gifts of food. Even if you don't have anyone in particular in mind when you buy an item that catches your eye, chances are when the holidays roll around, it will make a great fallback present. Also, try to collect things over the year. Is there a child on your list who loves coins, buttons, or matchbooks? How about seashells, playing cards, or rocks? Put these in a small display case and add a book on whatever it is the child is interested in, and you have a great, inexpensive Christmas gift.

Where can you buy gifts—*aside from* the malls? Check out the craft fairs that are held during the Christmas season. With goods made by local artisans, these can be a great source of inexpensive and unusual gifts. Look through your newspaper for notices about auctions and estate sales as well. You may be able to pick up prints, glassware, plates, or jewelry for people on your list. Also remember that you can get some of your shopping done at the many church and school bazaars held at Christmastime.

Books are great gifts. But don't limit yourself to shopping in the big bookstore chains. Secondhand bookstores are less expensive and often have out-of-print titles that can't be found in the big chains. Additionally, these stores may sell old prints or maps that you could frame for your family members or friends.

Hardware stores, housewares stores, and Asian import stores carry a wide variety of inexpensive houseware items. Consider such gifts as a set of plastic glasses for the patio, or a bunch of kitchen items like garlic presses, cheese knives, or wooden spoons you tie together with a red bow. This way, your friends will have all the utensils they need the next time they throw a dinner party.

Because catalogs are a convenient and increasingly popular source of gifts, one section of this chapter is devoted to mail-order retailers that sell practical and unusual gifts for $20 or less. Other sections are organized by the age group of the recipient, providing inexpensive gift suggestions for the children, teenagers, and adults on your Christmas list.

Mail-Order Gifts

Catalogs are a great source of gift ideas. During the holiday rush, many of these companies can save you time by wrapping and shipping the present for you. Shopping can be as simple as choosing the item and making a phone call. Of course, the wrapping costs a little extra, but the price may be worth the time you save.

If you'll be using direct mail, start early—as early as late October or early November. Many of these retailers require that the gift be ordered three weeks before Christmas to ensure it arrives on time, but if you wait that long, your item may be out of stock. So try to place your orders before Thanksgiving. If you're stuck, many direct-mail retailers will ship their goods via an express-mail service, but this can be expensive.

The following list is a short one. There are literally hundreds of direct-mail retailers in the United States and Canada. If you're interested in finding out about other catalogs, check your local library for indexes or associations of mail-order retailers. Or get a copy of the *Catalog Handbook* or *The Original Catalogue of Canadian Catalogues*. These publications are discussed below, followed by an alphabetical listing of specific catalogs.

The Catalog Handbook, Enterprise Magazines of Milwaukee; (414) 272-9977.

You can pick up this catalog at most magazine stands for $4. *The Catalog Handbook* doesn't sell anything; it just lists a lot of different catalogs that sell the items you may be looking for. Best of all, many of the entries are offbeat catalogs, like the one from Status for Sale — (800) 257-8288 — which sells nobility titles and backstage passes to concerts. A more conventional entry is that for Applesource — (217) 245-7589 — which sells eighty varieties of apples.

The Original Catalogue of Canadian Catalogues, by Leila Albala, Alpel Publishing, P.O. Box 203, Chambly, Quebec, Canada J3L 4B3; (514) 658-6205; fax (514) 658-3514.

With listings of more than 800 mail-order sources, this little book is a must for Canadian readers looking to avoid the crowds during the Christmas shopping season. The catalog provides its readers with sources for gifts ranging from religious articles to fly-fishing gear to products for left-handed people. Making the small investment in this book (C$9.95) can save you a lot of time and money. To order the next edition, give your name and address to the company; you'll be put on a mailing list and contacted when it's available.

American Spoon Foods, 1668 Clarion Avenue, P.O. Box 566, Petoskey, MI 49770-0566; (800) 222-5886.

The gift packs from American Spoon Foods take the hassle out of trying to find just the right present for adults on your list. This catalog offers mouthwatering assortments of jams, spoon fruits, salad dressings, and barbecue sauces. It's also a good source for holiday recipes. Pick a recipe you like, and send one of your friends a copy along with the mustard, dressing, or butter made by American Spoon Foods that's used in the recipe.

American Spoon Foods also sells dried fruits, marinades, pancake mixes, granola, and pasta sauces. Make a basket of your favorites to send to friends.

The Bird's Nest Mail Order, 331 Cornwallis Street, Kentville, Nova Scotia, Canada B4N 2G6; (902) 678-9514.

A good source of gifts for babies and toddlers, this catalog carries clothing, along with a number of items to decorate a child's room. It also features toys, books, and tapes for your children.

CD Plus Compact Disc Catalogue, 1825 Dundas Street East, Unit 13, Mississauga, Ontario, Canada L4X 2X1; (416) 629-9255; fax (416) 629-0414.

You can pick up this catalog at newsstands in Canada, or send C$4.95 to the above address to receive it. CD Plus carries over 27,000 music titles and will ship CDs anywhere in Canada.

Childcraft, P.O. Box 29149, Mission, KS 66201-9149; (800) 631-5667.

Those who need to buy gifts for children may be stumped during the holidays, either by the prices of games and toys, or by the overwhelming selection found in toy stores. Buying a child's gift through a catalog can make things a little easier on you, and many mail-order retailers like Childcraft will send the present to the recipient, wrapped and ready to go under the tree. The charge for this service typically runs between $2.50 to $5.00 per item.

Flax art & design, P.O. Box 7216, San Francisco, CA 94120-7216; (800) 547-7778.

There are a number of unusual items in this catalog that would make interesting Christmas gifts. How about an office alternative to the Swiss army knife? Flax sells an Ultra Portable Desk Tool, which is an eleven-in-one stationery organizer that contains, among other things, a ballpoint pen, hole punch, and tape measure. These and eight other gadgets are all found in this nifty $4\frac{1}{2}$-by-$1\frac{1}{2}$-inch design.

Gardeners Eden, Mail-Order Department, P.O. Box 7307, San Francisco, CA 94120-7307; (800) 822-9600.

This is a great source of gifts for the gardeners and plant lovers on your list. Those who live in apartments may appreciate a set of four brightly colored terra-cotta pots to put on their windowsill. For families who have big yards and like poppies, consider the Gardeners Eden's poppy bouquet, a seed mixture of poppies and Bishops Lace that can cover up to 200 square feet. The catalog also offers a Fragrant Flower seed mixture.

HearthSong, 156 North Main Street, Sebastopol, CA 95472; (800) 325-2502.

For the children on your list, this catalog is an excellent source of inexpensive but unusual gifts. While you can buy traditional toys like blocks and modeling beeswax, Hearthsong also sells books and craft kits, many of them for under $20.

Hold Everything, Mail-Order Department, P.O. Box 7807, San Francisco, CA 94120-7807; (800) 421-2264.

A good place to find gifts for the young adult who might need some things for his or her new apartment. The gadgets sold may not be at the top of anyone's Christmas list, but they are especially useful. Items include everything from floral storage boxes to plastic bags for storing sweaters or bedding.

The King Arthur Flour Baker's Catalogue, P.O. Box 876, Norwich, VT 05055-0876; (800) 827-6836.

For the adults or families on your Christmas list who love to cook, consider a gift from this catalog. It has everything from cookbooks to cookie cutters, flour, and pans.

Lillian Vernon, Virginia Beach, VA 23479-0002; (800) 285-5555.

This catalog carries clothes, jewelry, housewares, and children's toys—all at reasonable prices. Though the gifts may not be the most unusual, Lillian Vernon is still a great source for standbys. Little luxuries like a silver tissue holder and mirror, silk-covered pens from India, personalized business card cases, and traveling jewelry cases can all be ordered through the catalog. In addition, it has a wide range of goods for the home, such as a personalized door knocker, a tool organizer, and an adjustable wooden book rack for cookbooks.

Mountain Equipment Co-op, Department MCT, 1655 West Third Avenue, Vancouver, British Columbia, Canada V6J 1K1; (800) 663-2667.

Sells everything for the outdoor enthusiast, ranging from camping, hiking, and cycling equipment and clothing to books and other necessities.

Pocket Songs, 50 Executive Boulevard, Elmsford, NY 10523-1325; (800) NOW-SING.

This catalog has the perfect gift for the music lovers on your list. With 1,100 tapes and CDs to choose from, it is a gold mine of presents for families, adults, and teenagers. Pocket Songs sells tapes and CDs that let you remove the vocalist from the song and become the singer. They can be used with a karaoke machine or a cassette player. On one side, the tape has the complete recording, but the vocalist can be silenced by turning down the right speaker of your sound system. The second side features the same music minus the vocalist.

Pottery Barn, Mail-Order Department, P.O. Box 7044, San Francisco, CA 94120; (800) 922-5507.

A great source for inexpensive but trendy housewares. Miniature lanterns, votive candleholders, and sets of glassware are all priced under $20. The Pottery Barn also sells hurricane lamps to hang out on one's patio at night, napkin rings to dress up a table, a wrought iron wine rack, and a variety of glass bottles all within your Christmas budget.

Rand McNally, Attn.: Map and Atlas Customer Service, P.O. Box 7600, Chicago, IL 60680; (800) 333-0134.

This publisher of maps and atlases is a great gift source for both adults and children. Friends planning trips would love a *Road Atlas and Travel Guide*, which includes all kinds of vacation-planning information. Have a baseball fan on your list? *The Official Baseball Atlas* is a sports and travel guide that directs you through the cities and stadiums of the twenty-eight teams in the Major League. It also includes schedules for the teams' spring-training and regular seasons.

The Right Start Catalog, Right Start Plaza, 5334 Sterling Center Drive, Westlake Village, CA 91361-4627; (800) LITTLE-1.

This catalog will help you if you're trying to find gifts for your littlest nephews and nieces. It also sells goods that would be welcomed by any new or expectant parents on your list. Insulated tote bags for bottles, the Right Start's Thermal Container, which comes with a lid that conceals both a fork and spoon, and a thinsulate-lined pouch that keeps up to four bottles cold are great gifts for new parents on the go. Teething rings, hats, bath accessories, tapes, and videos are all available.

Road Runner Sports, 6310 Nancy Ridge Drive, Suite 101, San Diego, CA 92121; (800) 551-5558.

Shorts, T-shirts, racing singlets, and socks are all suitable gifts for the runner, active teenager, or weekend athlete on your list.

In addition to clothing, the catalog sells a number of items that would be welcomed by any athlete, like a Jogman, a carrying case for a Sony walkman, and a Neoprene Jog Bag, which is a waterproof case for carrying a portable cassette player.

The catalog also carries gear for swimmers, like goggles and swim caps, and other fitness equipment, such as back supports, chin-up bars, and a Cool Sports Bandanna to keep you cool during the warm weather.

Stocking Fillas, Ltd., 133 The West Mall Department AP-1, Unit 5, Toronto, Ontario, Canada M9C 5M7; (416) 621-6100, fax (416) 621-6599.

Stocking Fillas features a wide variety of toys, games, and other playthings for children, all within your budget.

Williams-Sonoma, Mail-Order Department, P.O. Box 7456, San Francisco, CA 94120-7456; (800) 541-2233.

Another excellent source of gifts for the cooks on your list, Williams-Sonoma sells a number of goods appropriate for families or adults who need to have their kitchenware "updated."

Worldwide Games, P.O. Box 517, Colchester, CT 06415-0517; (800) 888-0987.

This catalog has gifts for any person on your list. In addition to a wide variety of puzzles and board games, Worldwide Games sells items like an automatic card shuffler and wooden card holders. *The Backyard Games Book* is great for families with young children. Worldwide Games also sells kites and favorite games like Tiddly Winks.

Gifts for Children

More than any other holiday, Christmas belongs to children. Their excitement about the holiday reminds adults how magical the season can be. When you begin buying presents for the children on your list, try to remember which gifts you treasured most as a child. While some people may tell you that a child will only be satisfied with the latest, greatest, and most expensive toy, the child could be just as pleased with a video of his or her favorite Christmas movie, like *Rudolph the Red-Nosed Reindeer* or *How the*

Grinch Stole Christmas. And if you promise the child a trip to the ballpark to see a pro baseball game or a camping trip when the weather gets warmer, the gift not only would be within your budget but would provide great memories for the youngster.

Keep in mind the child's hobbies and special interests. Is he or she an avid artist or baseball lover? Thinking about these things will help you select an appropriate gift.

If you have no idea what to get a particular child, contact the battery manufacturer Duracell's Toy Hot Line, which offers gift suggestions. The phone number is (800) BEST-TOYS. If you know what toy you want to get the child and it happens to be made by Playskool, call (800) PLAYSKL for the name of the retailer nearest you.

Parenting magazines, *Consumer Reports,* or your local newspapers often feature articles on the best toys for kids, providing many ideas about what to get a child for Christmas.

Since finding the perfect gift for a child can be both mind-numbing and expensive, the suggestions that follow are intended to simplify your holiday shopping while keeping you within your Christmas budget.

Books, as well as books on tape, are always welcome presents.

Ask librarians or grade-school teachers to recommend some of the more popular ones.

Your post office carries beginner stamp-collector kits for children. The Canada Post Corporation sells stamp kits along with coins and other products geared toward the young philatelist on your list. For more information, write to Canada Post Corporation, National Philatelic Centre, Antigonish, Nova Scotia, Canada B2G 2R8; or call (800) 565-4363.

Don't throw out your old baseball cards; they might be a welcome addition to some youngster's collection.

Old-fashioned games like Chinese checkers, chess, jacks, marbles, and dominoes are perennial favorites. Game Entertainment, made by Capital, Inc., has equipment for playing checkers, cards, dominoes, chess, dice games, and backgammon.

Hand puppets are another good choice for young children. Folkman makes a variety of these.

If the youngster likes to jump rope, get one for the child, along with a book with different jump-roping rhymes. Other toys that encourage physical activity include the Woosh Flying Ring by Oddz on Products. And don't forget frisbees, whiffle balls and bats, and Nerf games.

For artistic youngsters, your local craft store has everything from sketchpads and coloring books to pencils, markers, and paint kits. Look for beading and macramé kits, or buy an embroidery kit for youngsters who'd like to learn needlework. The Potterycraft Clay and Paint Kit by Tyco Toys lets children try their hand at making pottery, from the molding of the pot to the painting of the finished product.

Budding scientists would appreciate a collection of rocks or minerals from a natural history museum. Exploratory makes the Exploroscope, a handheld microscope; and Uncle Milton makes the Geotek portable microscope, which sells for under $20. HarperCollins Publishers sells an Environmental Detective Kit that contains the materials to test for acid rain or build ant farms and terrariums. The kit also comes with educational books and pamphlets that cover the various environmental problems our world faces today and suggest ways kids can help solve these problems. In Canada, a good source of gifts for young scientists is Le Naturaliste, a mail-order retailer selling products for bird watching, astronomy, and so forth. For a catalog, write to Le Naturaliste, 1990, boul. Charest o. #117, Quebec City, Quebec, Canada G1N 4K8; or call (800) 463-6848.

Games like Scattergories, Yahtzee, Monopoly, Scrabble, and Clue are great gifts not only for children or teenagers but for families. Keep in mind newer additions to the game world that come highly recommended from consumers groups like Parents' Choice and from children as well. Two games that are both challenging and fun are Where in the World Is Carmen San Diego? and Brain Quest. Both are made by University Games. An educational game perfect for a child just learning to count is Snail's Pace Race by Ravensburger. This game teaches children about counting and colors.

A deck of cards, along with a book on how to play different games, would be a good option, as are Slinkies, yo-yos, jigsaw puzzles, and horseshoes.

A child might also appreciate a different kind of Christmas gift, such as a day at the natural history museum, a sleigh ride after the first snow, or a ticket to a local production of *A Christmas Carol.* Trips to caves, doll museums, fire engine museums, nautical or whaling museums might also pique a child's interest. You could take a child to a parade; to a flea market; to car, boat, or game trade shows as well as to local sporting events or television shows.

Take some time to search your attic before you throw out old clothes. Do you know a child who might like a box of these for dress up? Add some stories or plays the child could act out using the clothing as costumes.

A child might treasure something as simple as a kite, with plenty of string and instructions. If you live near an open space, you might invite the child over for an afternoon of kite flying. Or give the child a rubber stamp with the child's name and address on it, along with some sticks of sealing wax and a stamp with the child's initials.

Many kids would love a baking or sewing kit. For young bakers, include a muffin pan, some premixed dried ingredients, measuring cups and spoons, and a couple of your own recipes or a book of recipes devoted to muffins. For sewers, the kit could include a precut pillow, some stuffing, and a needle and thread, or some patterns and fabric to make dolls' clothes or beanbags.

For young carpenters, put together a tool kit containing a small hammer, a little screwdriver, a tape measure, a right angle, some screws, nails, and instructions on how to make simple objects like boxes or bookends.

Check out novelty stores for trick items children can play with, like pop-up snakes, dribbling water glasses, and magic kits. A good source for these kinds of gifts is the Johnson Smith *Things You Never Knew Existed* catalog. It sells the *Handbook of Magic*, along with a number of tricks children might love to learn. For a catalog, call (813) 747-2356.

Other standby gift ideas: balls of different sizes and stuffed animals. For the girls on your list, buy bunches of hair ribbons, barrettes, and headbands.

Subscriptions to magazines are lasting Christmas presents. Consider, for instance, a year's subscription to *Boys' Life*. For information, write to Boys' Life, P.O. Box 152079, Irving, TX 75105-2079.

Consumer Reports publishes *Zillions*, which is a kind of junior *Consumer Reports*. It's an excellent gift for children ages eight to fourteen. Write to Consumer Reports, Subscription Department, P.O. Box 51777, Boulder, CO 80321-1777.

For young sports enthusiasts, there's *Sports Illustrated for Kids*. Call (800) 633-8628. And don't forget publications that focus on specific sports like biking or hiking or other activities.

Finally, check your local library for the names of publications in the fields of science or writing that are geared toward children.

Gifts for Teenagers

Shopping for a teenager can be difficult for a couple of reasons. First, that trendy gift you bought in the fall may be out of fashion by the time Christmas rolls around. Second, in this consumer-driven society, the teenager may already have everything you'd be able to afford. Though you'd like to be able to give the teen a CD player, it just may be out of your price range this year. But don't despair; even teenagers appreciate simpler gifts.

As with any age group, a number of gifts would always be welcomed by a teenager. Since most teenagers love to listen to music, a tape or CD is a logical choice. So is a gift certificate to a music store. If you have an extensive music collection, why not tape some of your own CDs for the teenager as a gift? Or give a box of blank tapes and let the teen decide what music to record. A book by the teenager's favorite author or on his or her favorite subject is another inexpensive yet thoughtful gift.

What is the teenager passionate about? Environmental causes? Sports? Politics? Consider a gift of a membership in a local or national club that supports causes or fields that the teen is interested in.

Frames, posters, scrapbooks, and photo albums are other perennial favorites. An address book would also make a good gift. A journal, accompanied by the memoir of a favorite public figure or author, would be appreciated by aspiring writers.

Other gift ideas for teenagers include day trips to museums, parks, nature preserves, or trade shows; tickets to concerts, local college sporting events, plays, or lectures; and gift certificates to the local movie theater.

If the teenager is athletic, sporting or workout equipment and clothes are good options: You could give jump ropes, squash, tennis, or racquet balls, baseballs or softballs, dumbbells, T-shirts, or shorts. Also consider giving a subscription to a magazine like *Runners World, Bicycling,* or *Outside.* Some teens might appreciate bicycle repair kits.

For the female teens on your list, put together a box full of hair accessories like scrunchies, barrettes, combs, and clips. You could also give jars of potpourri or a certificate for a manicure. Check out secondhand stores for coats, scarves, hats, or jewelry, which many teens would welcome as additions to their wardrobe.

If you have a particular talent, why not offer a set of lessons for Christmas? Provided, of course, that he or she is interested in learning how to paint, play an instrument, or cook a certain cuisine.

Give the teen a certificate for driving lessons or a lesson in simple car repair or maintenance. If you have a video camera and the teen is a budding filmmaker, loan the camera for a couple of days of shooting.

In addition to the sports magazines mentioned earlier, the following publications would all be suitable for teenagers:

Essence
P.O. Box 53400
Boulder, CO 80322-3400
(800) 274-9395

Popular Mechanics
P.O. Box 7170
Red Oak, IA 51591
(800) 333-4948

Rolling Stone
Publishers Voice 150
29225 Chagrin Boulevard
Cleveland, OH 44122
(800) 568-7655

Sassy
P.O. Box 57503
Boulder, CO 80322-7503
(800) 274-2622

Seventeen
P.O. Box 55195
Boulder, CO 80322-5195
(800) 388-1749

Sierra
Sierra Club
730 Polk Street
San Francisco, CA 94109
(415) 776-2211

Gifts for Adults

Adults can often be the most difficult people on your list to buy for, in part because they seem to have everything, but also because they may be reluctant to give you a Christmas "wish list." Although many practical gifts might be out of your price range, a lot of inexpensive items would make their lives a little easier.

If you're unsure what to buy a certain adult on your list, look around that person's home on your next visit. And when he or she is rummaging around the kitchen or garage for some gadget or utensil, keep your ears open for a remark like, "Oh, I need to buy one." Also keep in mind the interests, hobbies, or avocations of the individual. What type of music does this person listen to?

What's his or her favorite cuisine? Narrowing your focus will make it easier to decide what to buy.

Some little things that make great gifts include soaps, a nice pen, and a spill-free coffee mug for the car. Throw in some special coffees with the mug for a more substantial gift.

Ideas for those who drive a lot: books on tape, maps, change holders for tolls, a rack for audiocassettes or CDs, and a tire repair kit.

For the frequent flyers on your list, you can purchase a few inexpensive items that might make their travel time less stressful. These include a travel iron, clothesline, or folding hangers. Those who go abroad would appreciate books on the cities they're visiting, tip purses filled with different currencies, or phrase books. One creative option is the Quickpoint Visual Translator, a fold-up card the size of an airline ticket that features more than 400 universally recognized drawings, depicting everything from ordering a steak to calling a doctor. Call 800-962-4943 to order.

A long plane ride might be more comfortable if the passenger had an inflatable neck rest or pillow, eye shades, or a couple of favorite tapes to play on his or her Walkman.

Checkbook holders and purses for small change or tokens are

great for daily outings. Keep in mind key rings, credit-card holders, and tote bags as well.

Campers on your list might like a little luxury in their lives when they're spending a night under the stars. GSI Outdoors sells a mini espresso maker. For more information, call (619) 271-7816. On cold nights, they'd appreciate a pair of Feet Heaters; these fleece socks will keep a person warm even when they're wet. They're made by Wyoming Woolens. Call (800) 732-2991.

You can enroll any person over the age of fifty as a member of the American Association of Retired Persons (AARP). Members get discounts on a number of goods and services. Write to AARP Membership Processing Center, P.O. Box 199, Long Beach, CA 90848-9983; or call (202) 434-2277.

If the adults on your list have other special interests or hobbies, a membership in a local or national club is a good gift idea. Your local library has a reference book entitled *Encyclopedia of Associations* that lists special-interest organizations by subject.

Gardeners on your list might appreciate a variety of bulbs or seeds from your local nursery. Look for gardening gloves or special tools they might need. A gift of waterproof plant markers would help them keep track of the perennials in their garden.

Gardener's Supply, a direct-mail retailer, sells a set of twenty-five of these. Call (802) 863-1700.

Prints or old maps from thrift shops, rummage sales, or local museums make great gifts. If you're in Washington D.C., check out the National Archives for its wealth of reproduction drawings, engravings, photographs, and old documents dealing with every facet of U.S. history and life. Framed, these make lovely presents. Purdham, a Canadian mail-order retailer, sells a wide variety of reproductions of maps and historical documents. In addition, it sells replicas of antique cars and trains, which could be a great gift for a friend who's an avid collector. For a catalog, write to Purdham, 3039 du Portage, Carignan, Quebec, Canada J3L 2B8. Canadian residents should include a self-addressed stamped envelope; from the United States, add a $2 check for postage and handling.

Letter writers on your list would appreciate more stationery, a clipboard, or a box containing pens, pencils, stamps, and airmail stickers. Address labels, a rubber address stamp and ink pad, postcards, correspondence cards, or an address book would all be welcome gifts.

For the chefs on your list, cookbooks are a sure choice. Give books on different cuisines, and make each gift that much more special by including some of the special and unusual spices these recipes call for. You could also buy the cook pots of fresh herbs and include directions on how to dry them and recipes the herbs are used in. If you have a group of friends who are avid cooks, why not get together and exchange five of your favorite recipes as Christmas gifts? Each friend would buy a recipe box, place five recipes in it, and present it to another member of the group. In addition, they'd provide copies of the recipes for all the other members of the group. The box would then be filled by the recipes each person receives from his or her group of friends.

Put together coffee and tea samplers for your relatives. You can buy both in bulk and put them in jars and containers you've collected throughout the year. Label each container with a description of the coffee or tea, and place the samples in a wooden box or tray.

Young adults who've just moved into their first apartment probably need a number of things to make their kitchen functional. Give them a book of your recipes or a couple of basic cookbooks. Heavy-duty can or bottle openers, knives, and cutting boards are also useful. You could make a little toolbox for them; fill it with nails, picture hooks, a hammer, and a screwdriver.

Some kitchen appliances are not as expensive as you might think. Black and Decker sells a Handy Juicer, and Hamilton Beach has fairly inexpensive blenders. Two reasonably priced mixers are the Moulinex Max-Chopper and the Black and Decker HC20. If you want to go in on a gift with another friend, why not buy a Crockpot?

Buy a bunch of mason jars and fill them with different kinds of pasta, candies, nuts or sunflower seeds, or something you made yourself like apple butter, jellies, or different sauces. By doing this, you can finish off a lot of your Christmas shopping with a single trip to the grocery store and an afternoon at home preparing the goods.

Like the children and teenagers on your list, adults would enjoy a subscription to a magazine. Many people are becoming concerned about saving money for retirement or for their children's college education. They might appreciate a subscription to a magazine like *Kiplinger's Personal Finance Magazine* or *Money*. You could also buy a ledger that would help them keep track of their savings, investments, and taxes.

You can be a bit more creative with family gifts. Many times a present to a group of people can be something you made yourself, like a batch of cookies in a tin or a special Christmas basket filled with ornaments and food. For family gifts, there are always such standbys as coffee-table books, videos, and games, which everyone can enjoy. Consider indoor games like Risk, backgammon, checkers, or puzzles and outdoor games like badminton, horseshoes, or a volleyball net and ball. Holiday-related items like a Christmas tablecloth, a set of Christmas coffee mugs, or a set of holiday glasses are other safe bets.

Gifts for the home, such as personalized stationery with the family's address on it, or welcome mats for the front door would be appreciated. For people with patios and pools, purchase items they can use when the weather is warm. Small plastic tables, plastic tumblers or serving trays, and citronella candles are perfect for use outside. Rafts, floating games, and inflatable balls to toss around can all be used in the pool.

Throughout the year, keep your eye out for inexpensive wicker baskets. Fill little ones with bulbs of garlic or packages of fresh herbs for the family's kitchen. In bigger baskets, put dishtowels or soaps for the family's bathroom.

Families traveling with a newborn would appreciate a baby traveling kit. Include a plastic-lined bag with disposable diapers, a bottle warmer, formula, baby toy, towelettes, a teething ring, spoon, and a jar or two of baby food.

You can also give families subscriptions to a magazine like *National Geographic, Consumer Reports, Yankee Magazine, Reader's Digest,* or one of the many publications that focuses on the city they live in (e.g., *New York, Philadelphia, Chicago, Toronto Life*).

Gifts for the Vision Impaired

There are a number of places from which you can order Christmas gifts for the vision impaired. First and foremost would be Books on Tape, which carries a large selection of audio books. Write to Books on Tape, P.O. Box 7900, Newport Beach, CA 92660; or call (800) 252-6996.

G. K. Hall and Co. has a catalog featuring Large Print Books. For a copy, write to Large Print Books, 70 Lincoln Street, Boston, MA 02111; or call (800) 257-5755.

The American Printing House for the Blind sells braille books. Write to the American Printing House for the Blind, P.O. Box 6085, Louisville, KY 40206; or call (800) 223-1839.

Lastly, the *New York Times* prints a weekly, large-type newspaper. To order, write to the *New York Times,* Mail Subscriptions, P.O. Box 9564, Uniondale, NY 11556-9564; or call (800) 631-2580.

Along the same lines, why not make your own tape of a book and present it as a gift to someone you know who is vision impaired?

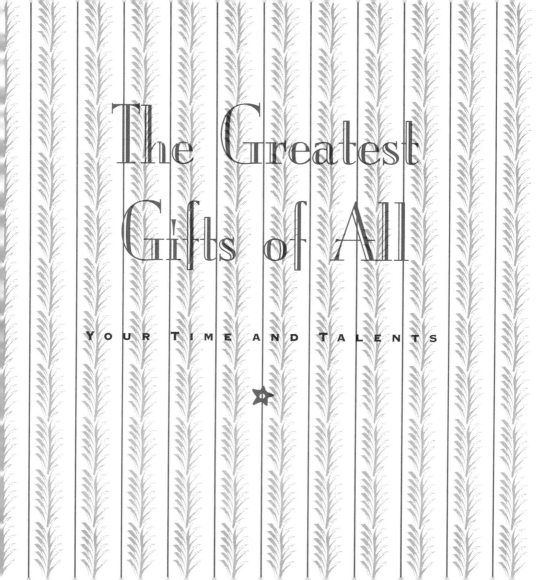

The Greatest Gifts of All

Your Time and Talents

More often than not, the mall or nearest shopping strip isn't the best place to find a meaningful gift for someone. If there's someone special on your list, consider giving something of yourself: your time or your talents. The possibilities are endless. You can offer to baby-sit a newborn or give cookies, homemade jam or jelly, an original painting, embroidered pillow or hand-knit scarf, sweater, hat, or mittens.

You know what you're good at; go with it. On the other hand, if you don't have the time to make something before Christmas, or if you don't think you have any particular talents that might translate into a gift, consider giving the gift of your time—in the form of a homemade coupon. These days, our lives are so busy with work, family, and just getting little things in order that time has become a precious commodity.

The coupon itself can be rather simple: a handwritten note or card with your offer penned inside. Or you could design one, using magazine pictures and words. Come up with an idea, then cut out appropriate images. Mount them on the back of a large index card or piece of white paper. If you'd like to take an art lover to a museum exhibit or gallery, for example, clip images of famous works from an art magazine. If you're taking someone to a movie, snip quotes from recent reviews of current movies.

Some possibilities for coupons:

❄ Spend an afternoon with a child on your list. Plan a trip to a destination—perhaps a movie or play—the child selects. Or take the child for an ice-cream sundae. One great afternoon could mean a lot more than a toy or new clothes.

❄ Offer to baby-sit for a couple who doesn't get out much. Give them a booklet of baby-sitting certificates good for several nights of the year (perhaps their anniversary or a birthday). Chances are this would be a treasured gift.

❄ If one of your elderly relatives is in a nursing home or can't get out of the house very often, why not serve as a chauffeur for a day? Take your relative to the mall so he or she can do some shopping without worrying about transportation.

❄ If you're handy around the house, offer your services to a friend who needs something repaired.

❄ The artistically gifted could give a child drawing or painting lessons for a specified amount of time.

❄ Volunteer to help a family with a big project, like painting a room or doing yard work in the spring.

❋ Cook someone his or her favorite dinner. The recipient might freeze it for another night or eat it on the spot—and you would clean up afterward. Some parents would probably love a night away from the kitchen.

❋ Give the gift of transportation if you have a car and a friend doesn't. A box of coupons could entitle a friend to use your driving services on several occasions.

❋ City dwellers would probably appreciate a weekend in the country or suburbs. If you live outside a metropolitan area, consider inviting city rats to your neck of the woods. And vice-versa: If you live in the city, invite country friends out for a weekend of shopping, plays, and museums.

❋ Help someone who's throwing a party. Offer to serve food, tend bar, run errands, or clean up afterward.

❋ If you know someone who will be alone during the holidays, extend an invitation to share in your family's festivities.

❋ Massages are always much appreciated. With the variety of aromatherapy oils on the market, you should be able to give a good rub to someone who's especially stressed out at work.

❋ Take a friend to a movie or show he or she has been dying to see. Offer to pay for popcorn.

Children can also create coupons (with magazine pictures, drawings, or paintings). Some suggestions for youngsters:

❄ Offer to do a chore without being asked; read a story to a younger sibling; sort a mess in the kitchen cabinet; return a brother's books to the library; or clean a sister's room (of course, certain areas might be off-limits).

❄ Spend time with a brother, sister, mother or father—doing what they like best. Go shopping or to a basketball game. Play golf or Scrabble.

❄ Think about what someone really needs, then offer a specific "service." If someone frequently travels out of town on business, you might want to offer to pick up his or her mail each day. You may also know someone without the time or inclination to do the dirty work around the house. Offer to clean a fish tank or litter box.

❄ Spend time with the new kid on the block. Take him or her to the movies or go bowling. Holidays and vacations can be especially lonely for a newcomer.

Naturally, children who are old enough may want to get their parents a Christmas present. Ask your parents for a small amount of money (or use your allowance!) and have them take you to the store. If you're creative, however, you may want to make something—a surprise. Special talents will come in handy: Budding photographers can snap a family portrait or beautiful scene, then frame it—either with an inexpensive store-bought frame or homemade one. Artistic types may want to paint a picture and frame it.

Kids, here are some other possibilities:

❆ Paperweights can be made from smooth stones and paints. Simply collect stones, wash them, and paint a design on the stone (a heart, a star, or a butterfly, for example).

❆ Create bookmarks with simple materials: metal hair clips or cardboard cut in long strips, glue, and glitter (or other decorating materials, such as felt). Glue on the glitter or felt or whatever you want.

❆ To make a memo clip, you'll need a clothespin, paint, beads, buttons or seashells, and small stickers (as well as glue). Paint the clothespin and glue the decorations on the pin's surface. Purchase a small note pad and attach it to the clip. Then write a message on the pad.

❆ Magnets are also easy to make. Buy a metal or plastic magnet (sold at dime stores), scraps of felt or other decorative materials, and glue. Just glue the items on top of each magnet.

❄ Stationery is also a useful and creative homemade gift. Draw designs on a piece of white paper folded in half. Then tie the paper together with colorful yarn, and include gold or silver seals or stickers.

❄ Make recipe cards for the cook in the family by drawing designs (perhaps pictures of the food) or pasting pictures from a food magazine on the blank side of lined index cards. Decorate an old file box to keep them in.

❄ An organizer is also a practical gift for most adults. Collect different sized cardboard boxes (preferably small ones, such as jewelry boxes and tissue paper tubes) and arrange them on the bottom of a big box (an empty typing paper box is perfect). Glue the bottoms of the little boxes inside the bottom of the big box, and spray-paint the sides; decorate with yarn, felt, or stickers.

❄ Make coloring books for your younger brothers and sisters: Draw pictures on white paper and consider writing a story to accompany them. For older siblings or other relatives, write stories and include illustrations or just an illustrated cover.

❄ Create a tie for Dad with Signals' Design a Tie kit, which comes with five magic markers and a practice swatch. Or personalize a plate or mug with the company's Make a Plate and Make a Mug sets. These can be ordered through Signals, WGBH Educational Foundation, P.O. Box 64428, St. Paul, MN 55164-0428; (416) 586-5842.

❆ For other ideas, scan *Highlights* magazine or library books. The gift-making possibilities are endless.

Gifts of food, of course, are another option—for adults and children alike. Maybe you have a special recipe for Christmas cookies that's been handed down through the generations. If so, make up a batch and give them to your friends along with a copy of the recipe. Or prepare a variety of foods and put them in a little basket with an ornament hanging from the handle.

As mentioned earlier in the book, even if you don't have any particular family food traditions, you can adopt some. What follows are a few favorite family recipes, as well as recipes for treats served around the world during Christmastime. Any of these foods would make a unique Christmas gift. Prepare these recipes early in the season, then put together baskets of goodies for family and friends.

Piernik (Honey Spice Cake)

A popular dish at Christmastime in Poland, *piernik* is said to promote intelligence, good health, and good luck.

5 cups flour	1 teaspoon baking soda
2 cups sugar	1/4 teaspoon cream of tartar
1 cup honey	1/2 teaspoon cloves
1/2 cup butter	1/4 teaspoon cinnamon
1/4 cup water	1/4 teaspoon nutmeg
2 eggs	

Melt 1 tablespoon sugar in a large skillet and allow it to caramelize. Pour in the water and allow it to boil. Add the rest of the sugar. When the sugar has dissolved, add the honey, cloves, cinnamon, and nutmeg. Allow this mixture to boil, then let it cool. Sift flour. Put aside one cup with which to flour the board. Add butter, eggs, flour, baking soda, and cream of tartar to the caramelized sugar mixture. Knead well, adding more flour to make elastic dough. Refrigerate dough for 30 minutes. Roll out on floured board. Bake at 350° for 15 minutes.

Source: *Treasured Polish Christmas Customs and Traditions, Carols,*

Decorations, and a Christmas Play. Minneapolis, Minn.: Polanie Publishing, 1972.

Panforte di Siena

This rich mixture of hazelnuts, almonds, citron, flour, cocoa, and spices has become synonymous with Christmas in Italy.

½ cup sugar
4 ounces honey
½ cup flour
2 tablespoons cocoa
1 tablespoon cinnamon
½ pound diced candied fruit

2 tablespoons diced citron
¼ pound toasted shelled almonds
¼ pound toasted shelled hazelnuts
1 tablespoon grated orange rind
powdered sugar

Mix sugar and honey in saucepan; cook over low flame for 10 minutes, stirring constantly with wooden spoon. Cover saucepan and remove from fire.

Sift together flour, cocoa, and cinnamon in a bowl. Gradually stir into honey and sugar mixture. Place over very low flame; stir in candied fruit and citron. Fold in nuts and orange rind. Blend; remove from heat. Pour quickly into buttered 10-inch pie plate.

Bake in slow oven (275°) for 30 minutes, or until firm. Remove from oven and cool. Sprinkle heavily with powdered sugar. Cut into serving pieces.

Source: *The Art of Making Italian Desserts*, by Maria LoPinto. Garden City, N.Y.: Doubleday, 1952.

Plum Pudding

Try this classic English Christmas dish for a festive new twist at your holiday table.

1½ pounds seedless raisins	*¾ pound bread crumbs*
½ pound currants	*8 eggs*
¾ pound beef suet	*2 wineglasses of brandy*
½ pound mixed candied orange, lemon, and apple peels	

Cut the raisins in half, but don't chop them. Wash, pick, and dry the currants. Mince the suet finely. Cut the candied peels into thin slices and grate the bread into fine crumbs. When all these dry ingredients are prepared, mix them, then moisten the mixture with the eggs, which should be well beaten, and add one glass of brandy. Stir well and press the pudding into a greased pudding mold. Cover tightly and boil for 5 or 6 hours. When you take the pudding out of the pot, put a saucer underneath to catch the water that may drain from it. The day it is to be eaten, plunge the pudding into boiling water for at least two hours. Then take the pudding out of the mold, pour a glass of brandy around it, light with a match, and serve the dish encircled in flame.

Adapted from: *Brandreth's Christmas Book*. New York: Van Nostrand Reinhold, 1975.

Marzipan

Christmas wouldn't be the same without this festive German candy.

½ pound almonds   *1 egg yolk*
1 egg white   *½ pound powdered sugar*
1 tablespoon rose water

Grind the almonds twice in a food processor with a steel blade. Mix with the egg white and rose water to form a smooth paste. Let stand overnight. Form little pretzels, rolls, and loaves out of this mixture. Brush with egg yolk and put on a baking tray covered with greaseproof paper. Cook at 350° for 12 to 14 minutes till the marzipan turns brown. Sprinkle the powdered sugar on top.

Source: *Christmas in Germany*. Bonn, Germany: Hohwacht Verlag, 1978.

Divinity Bars

This delicious white fudge is savored each year by the Shippey and Pike families in New Jersey. It has been passed down through four generations.

2¹/₂ cups sugar　　　　　*¹/₂ cup coarsely chopped walnuts*
¹/₂ cup water　　　　　*1 teaspoon vanilla*
¹/₂ cup white Karo syrup
2 egg whites beaten to soft peaks
　(and sitting at room
　temperature)

Boil the sugar, water, and syrup till this mixture turns into soft balls. Pour half of the mixture over the beaten egg whites, a little at a time. Stir. Cook the rest of the syrup till it turns into hard balls. Beat the egg-white mixture and slowly add the hard ball syrup. Continue beating until the mixture no longer appears shiny. Add nuts and vanilla, pour onto a lightly greased pan or drop by the teaspoon onto buttered plates, and wait a few hours for the fudge to harden.

Chocolate Dip Balls

For chocolate and peanut butter lovers everywhere, this recipe is another favorite of the Shippey family.

3/4 cup peanut butter
1 cup powdered sugar
1 cup coconut
1/2 cup chopped nuts
1 cup chopped dates

1/4 teaspoon salt
1 teaspoon vanilla
1 egg, beaten
6-ounce package of chocolate bits
1/4 of a paraffin brick

Combine the peanut butter and sugar. Add coconut, nuts, dates, salt, and vanilla. Mix in beaten egg. Shape into balls.

Melt the entire package of chocolate bits in a double boiler. Dip the "balls" in the melted chocolate and place on wax paper to cool.

Missing Chocolate Square Cookies

A favorite of the Gilbert family of Philadelphia, this recipe was missing from the family archives for some time until it was rediscovered a few years ago. These squares are a great treat for the chocolate lovers on your list.

17 unsugared graham crackers,
  crumbled
²/₃ cup broken walnuts

1 cup condensed milk
16-ounce package of chocolate
  chips

Crumble all ingredients together and mix. Spread mixture into a well-greased 8- × -8-inch pan. Bake at 350°F for 20 minutes. Cut into squares.

Diane's Special Syrups

These delicious toppings, served over ice cream or sponge cakes, are a perfect way to end a festive holiday dinner.

Use any combination of:
Strawberries and rum

Cherries and brandy
Raspberries and cognac

First make a sugar syrup by combining 1 cup of sugar and 1 cup of water Heat the mixture to 230°F.

Add the liquor of choice, mixing one part alcohol with one part syrup. Pour this liquid over the fruit, which has been packed into clean glass jars. Seal and store in a cool place for two months. Refrigerate the sauces once they've been opened.

A couple of tips when making these sauces: Run the glasses through the dishwasher before you pack them with fruit, and make sure the fruit is clean.

Mab's Pepper Jelly

For many years, Mary Anne Burns, or Mab, has been making her pepper jelly at Christmastime for her group of friends. Served on crackers covered with cream cheese, this red or green jelly makes a delightful holiday hors d'oeuvre.

½ cup jalapeno peppers, seeded
  and ground

¾ cup bell or red peppers, seeded
  and ground

6½ cups sugar
1½ cups apple cider vinegar
6-ounce package of Certo pectin

Red or green food coloring (only two to three drops)
8 ½-pint sterile jelly glasses

Combine peppers, sugar, and vinegar, and bring to a hard boil, stirring constantly. Add pectin and food coloring, and bring to a second, hard, rolling boil. Boil for 1 minute. Remove and let stand for 5 minutes. Skim the foam off the top, being careful not to remove the peppers. Fill jelly glasses to within ⅛ to ¼ inch from the top. Seal and place upside down for 5 minutes. Check the seal in 1 hour to make sure the "pop" is down.

English Tea Cakes

The smell of these English tea cakes warming in the oven will get any weary adult out of bed on Christmas morning. This treat is a festive way to start the holiday when served with a big cup of hot coffee, cocoa, or tea.

3 eggs
1 cup sugar
1 cup melted butter

3 yeast cakes dissolved in 2 cups lukewarm water
½ pound golden raisins

4 tablespoons orange peel   *1 teaspoon nutmeg*
1 teaspoon salt   *10 cups sifted flour*

Combine all ingredients, and let the dough rise. Knead the dough, split it evenly, put it in two greased 9-inch round pans, and let it rise again. Spread the dough in each pan, and bake at 375°F for 10 minutes. Let the cakes cool, then remove them from the pans. Split them horizontally. Put the bottom of each back in its pan and spread with the following, creamed together:

³/₄ pound butter
1 pound confectioners' sugar

Place the top back on each cake, and bake at 300°F for 25 minutes. Cut each cake into eight pieces, and serve warm.

Herb Vinegar/Garlic Vinegar

These vinegars are lovely additions to any Christmas basket. Tie a bright red ribbon around the necks of the bottles, and include a recipe that might call for one of the vinegars.

To prepare herb vinegar: Save wine or other narrow-necked

bottles and their corks. Scrub the corks clean, or use plastic-topped bottles that have been run through the dishwasher. Place 1 cup of a slightly crushed fresh herb, either tarragon, basil, dill, rosemary, parsley, or thyme, in a quart mason jar. Bring a quart of white or red wine vinegar to a boil, and pour it into the mason jar over the herb. Cap this mixture, and let it steep for two weeks. Then strain the liquid into the bottles, and put a fresh sprig of the herb in each and seal the bottle. If you cork the bottles, rather than using the plastic tops, dip the corks and the tops of the bottles in melted sealing or candle wax.

To make garlic vinegar: Put some cloves of garlic on a bamboo skewer, put the skewer and a quart of white or red vinegar in a mason jar, and let the liquid steep for two weeks. When making garlic vinegar, remember you don't need to heat the vinegar. After two weeks, strain the vinegar, seal, and label.

Bourbon Balls

These delicious, no-bake cookies are a welcome treat at Christmastime. Easy to make, they are a must for any bag of goodies you put together.

3 cups vanilla wafer crumbs (12-oz pkg.)	1/2 cup bourbon
1 cup chopped pecans	1/2 cup cocoa
3 tablespoons light corn syrup	A pinch of salt
	2 cups confectioners' sugar

Roll wafers to a fine crumb, or run through a food processor. Thoroughly blend crumbs, nuts, corn syrup, bourbon, cocoa, salt, and 1 cup of the confectioners' sugar. Form into balls, and roll each one twice in the remaining confectioners' sugar.

Candy-Stripe Twists

These cookies are a holiday favorite. Leave them straight or bend the ends so they look like candy canes.

3 1/4 cups flour	1 egg
4 teaspoons baking powder	1/2 teaspoon oil of anise
1 teaspoon salt	1/4 cup milk
1/2 cup butter or margarine	Red food coloring
1 1/4 cups sugar	

Sift together flour, baking powder, and salt. In a separate bowl cream together butter and sugar, then beat in the egg and the oil of anise. Add the dry ingredients to the creamed mixture, one-third at a time, alternating the dry ingredients with the milk. Blend well.

Once the ingredients are blended, split the dough in half and tint one half with red food coloring. Leave the other half plain. Pinch off a teaspoon of both the red and plain dough, and roll each until it is pencil thin and about 5 inches long. Place the ends of each of the strips together, and twist into a rope. Bake the twists on an ungreased cookie sheet at 350°F for about 10 minutes, or until they are firm. Do not brown.

Crescent Cookies

These cookies are a favorite of the Kahr family, who make them only at Christmastime at their home in Newton, Massachusetts. It's worth waiting a whole year to taste them.

1/2 pound butter or margarine
1/2 cup sugar
2 cups flour
2 cups chopped pecans

1 teaspoon vanilla
3 teaspoons water
Confectioners' sugar

Cream together butter and sugar. Add flour, chopped nuts, and vanilla. Mix well. Add water and mix until the ingredients no longer cling to the sides of the bowl. Shape the dough into crescents. Bake the cookies on an ungreased cookie sheet at 350°F for 12 to 15 minutes. Do not let the cookies brown. Sprinkle them in confectioners' sugar while they are still warm.

Glazed Lime Nut Bread

The following is a tasty change from the more traditional tea breads made with blueberries, poppyseeds, or cranberries.

1/4 pound butter
1 cup plus 2 tablespoons sugar
2 eggs
Grated peel from one lime
Juice from one lime

2 cups sifted all-purpose flour
2 1/2 teaspoons baking powder
1 teaspoon salt
3/4 cup milk
1/2 cup chopped walnuts

Cream together butter and 1 cup of the sugar until light and fluffy. Add eggs and lime peel and beat well. Next, add all but 2 teaspoons of the lime juice and mix well.

Sift together flour, baking powder, and salt, then add this to the creamed mixture, alternating with the milk. After each addition, beat the mixture until it's smooth. Stir in walnuts, and pour into a greased loaf pan measuring $9 \times 5 \times 2\frac{1}{2}$ inches.

Bake at 350°F for 50 to 55 minutes. Cool in the pan for about 10 minutes, then spoon the mixture of the 2 remaining teaspoons of lime juice and 2 tablespoons of sugar over the top. Remove from the pan and cool.

Lime Ginger Cookies

One can never have enough recipes for great-tasting cookies. The following is one the Caton family likes to use when they celebrate a Cape Cod Christmas at their home in West Barnstable, Massachusetts.

2 cups sifted flour
2 teaspoons baking powder
½ teaspoon salt (optional)
¼ teaspoon ginger
1 cup butter or butter-flavored
  Crisco

1¼ cups sugar
2 eggs
3 teaspoons lime zest
4 teaspoons lime juice

Sift together flour, baking powder, salt, and ginger. Cream together butter and sugar. Add eggs, lime zest, lime juice, and blend with dry ingredients. Refrigerate for a couple of hours.

When you bake these cookies, take out only enough dough for each cookie sheet; otherwise the dough will get too soft from being left out too long.

Drop level tablespoons or full teaspoons of the dough on an ungreased baking sheet. Press the dough down with a fork. Bake the cookies at 350°F for 10 to 12 minutes, or until they are lightly browned around the edges. Remove and cool on wire racks.

These cookies freeze very well. Frozen cookies should be taken out of the freezer and allowed to defrost for about 20 minutes to half an hour before serving. If you put them in a toaster oven at 275°F for about 8 minutes or so, the cookies will taste as though they were just baked.

Agnes Alexander's Oatmeal Cookies

Agnes Alexander's original recipe called for a half pound of lard. It was created at a time when people cooked with lard instead of shortening. Although the results were delicious, in light of our new health consciousness, the lard has been exchanged for short-ening.

1 cup shortening or butter-
    flavored Crisco
1 cup brown sugar
2 cups oatmeal
2 cups flour
1 teaspoon baking soda in ¼ cup
    water

½ teaspoon salt (optional)
2 teaspoons vanilla
2 or 3 tablespoons milk
1 heaping cup chopped nuts

Mix all the ingredients together. Drop heaping teaspoons of the dough on a greased cookie sheet, and press the dough down with a fork. Bake the cookies at 350°F to 375°F for 12 to 15 minutes. Remove and let cool.

Christmas 1995 has presented a number of suggestions for cele-brating the holidays in new and old-fashioned ways. Christmas is a wonderful time of the year; it's a shame to lose sight of its mes-sage of love, hope, and friendship in all the rush that surrounds it. So try to take a different approach to the holiday this year: Keep it simple, emphasize tradition, and do one thing—whether it's through a gift you buy or an event you attend—that will in some way help others who may not have the means to celebrate the holiday season.

Index